TRINITARIAN THEOLOGY
TODAY

TRINITARIAN THEOLOGY TODAY

ESSAYS ON DIVINE BEING AND ACT

Edited by

Christoph Schwöbel

for the

Research Institute in Systematic Theology

King's College, London

T&T CLARK
EDINBURGH

T&T CLARK LTD
59 GEORGE STREET
EDINBURGH EH2 2LQ
SCOTLAND

First published 1995

ISBN 0 567 09731 5

British Library Cataloguing-in-Publication Data
A catalogue record for this book is available from the British Library

Printed and bound in Great Britain by Bookcraft, Avon

Contents

Introduction
The Renaissance of Trinitarian Theology:
Reasons, Problems and Tasks

Christoph Schwöbel

One of the most interesting developments in systematic theology in recent years has been a renewed interest in the doctrine of the Trinity and its implications for various aspects of Christian theology. While at the beginning of this period it still seemed necessary to lament the neglect of trinitarian reflection in modern theology and to offer apologies for engaging with such allegedly remote and speculative issues, both, lamentation and apologies, would seem to be out of place in today's theological situation. There is a rich variety of proposals for conceiving and reconstructing the doctrine of the Trinity, ranging from new attempts at developing the so-called psychological model of the Trinity, focusing on the analogy of the divine trinitarian life with the unity and differentiation of human consciousness in its various acts, to conceptions proposing social models of the Trinity, oriented towards an exploration of the triune being as the being of persons in communion. Equally varied is the theological and methodological background of such reflections which can include such divergent conceptualities as that of liberation theology or of a Hegelian theory of the Absolute.

A characteristic feature of this increased engagement with the doctrine of the Trinity is that it is not restricted to specific issues of the Christian doctrine of God while leaving other aspects of theology unchanged. Reflection on the Trinity, so it seems, inevitably has repercussions for the whole project of Christian theology and its relation to the cultural situation of the times. Trinitarian theology therefore appears to be a summary label for doing theology that effects all aspects of the enterprise of doing theology in its various disciplines. Because of this it is difficult to point to any one area of theological reflection that is not potentially affected by being viewed from a trinitarian perspective. This concerns not only major doctrinal topics such as the doctrine of creation, the destiny of humankind, the person and work of Christ, the church, its ministries and sacraments, and eschatology, but also those areas where doctrinal reflection and non-theological modes of inquiry overlap, such as the conversation with the natural sciences, anthropological inquiries, historical investigation and social theory. In being relevant for the main doctrinal topics trinitarian theology also affects the interface these topics have with non-theological forms of inquiry.

One reason for the wide-ranging potential implications of the doctrine of the Trinity for various aspects of theology is that this doctrine has a different status from other doctrines. It does not easily fit into the traditional order of dogmatic *loci*, roughly following, as they are, the narrative sequence of salvation history. The peculiar status of this doctrine is one point, almost the only point, where the two antipodes of modern theology, Friedrich Schleiermacher and Karl Barth, agree. It is this recognition of the special status of Trinity discourse that led both not to attempt finding a place for the doctrine within the framework of dogmatic *loci* but to develop its significance in the *epilegomena* in Schleiermacher's case and in the *prolegomena* in Barth's. However different their views on the assessment of the doctrine of the Trinity were, they nevertheless agreed that Trinity discourse relates to the shape and structure of the whole framework of Christian doctrine and therefore cannot be presented as one doctrine within that framework. Because of this any theological decision taken with regard to the doctrine of the Trinity will have echoes throughout the whole building of Christian doctrinal theology.

We have already mentioned that this new interest in the doctrine of the Trinity is neither restricted to a particular school of theology nor to a specific intellectual tradition. What is perhaps more important is that it also not limited to a particular ecclesial or confessional tradition. The resurgence of interest in trinitarian theology can claim to be taking up some of the seminal insights and proposals of three of the most influential theologians of an earlier generation, Karl Barth, Karl Rahner and Vladimir Lossky, each representing major ecclesial traditions. The most significant studies on trinitarian theology that have shaped the debate in recent years show that the theological impetus of trinitarian thinking has spread into all major denominations. In spite of the diversity of their trinitarian conceptions these theologians agree in seeing trinitarian theology as the primary orientation for their work. It is interesting to note that the points of agreement, shared emphases and different accents that are documented in these studies cannot easily be traced back to the ecclesial background or denominational allegiance of their authors. At a time when the prospects for an advance of ecumenism towards greater institutional church unity seem decidedly gloomy, albeit sometimes for good reasons, there appears in some theological quarters the possibility of a shared appreciation of trinitarian theology that cannot remain without effect for the way in which the churches learn to conceive the way towards greater communion.

When one considers the factors and motives that can be identified as having contributed to this increased interest in trinitarian theology one encounters a diverse, multifaceted bundle of factors, some of them connected to specific historical developments in the situation of the churches, others bound up with issues of an explicitly doctrinal character and others related to the situation of Christian faith in its cultural context. One of the major influences for an increasing awareness of the significance of trinitarian questions in theology and in the life of the church in Western churches is without doubt the encounter with Eastern Orthodoxy, its liturgy and its theology, in the ecumenical context. At the outset this encounter focused almost exclusively on the *filioque* as the doctrinal difference that led to different forms of theology, liturgical practice and spirituality. However, it soon became clear that the *filioque* does not simply represent the demarcation line between Eastern and Western trinitarianism. It could only have this divisive effect because it concentrates as in a magnifying glass the different perspectives of Eastern and Western views of the Trinity. The criticism of Western trinitarianism by Eastern Orthodox theologians can be summarized in the view that the Western view of the Trinity building on the *filioque* jeopardizes the full equality of the third person and leads to a wholly problematical Christomonism in theology, spirituality and in the understanding of the church. However, this sort of criticism, offered perhaps in its most succinct and therefore occasionally harshest form by Vladimir Lossky, can only be understood against the background of an understanding of God where the Trinity summarizes what can theologically be said about God, and where the persons of the Trinity understood in an ontological sense as a communion of *hypostaseis* are the beginning and end of trinitarian discourse. Viewed in this way the debate about the *filioque* quickly demonstrates that the issue at stake concerns the *person* of the Holy Spirit that seems to be inadequately expressed in Latin trinitarianism and therefore the significance of the trinitarian conception of personhood in general. The ecumenical encounter with Eastern Orthodoxy brought Western theologians therefore from the question of the *filioque* into the heart of Eastern trinitarianism shaped by the seminal insights of the Cappadocians concerning the ontology of personhood.

The main upshot of this encounter is a very simple truth. It consists in the discovery that the doctrine of the Trinity matters. It is not a topic reserved for austere theological speculation or the language and practice of worship. The conceptual form in which the doctrine of the Trinity is expressed will affect not only the content and emphases of the doctrinal scheme of theology but also the forms of community organization in the church and its life of worship. The questioning of pneuma-tological, christological and ecclesiological tenets of the Western tradition by theologians representing the Eastern tradition appear in the ecumenical encounter between East and West as intrinsically connected with the different forms of trinitarian doctrine represented by both traditions. Coming to a better mutual understanding in ecumenical dialogue therefore requires to trace the points where the theological traditions of the Eastern and the Western churches diverge in their understanding of the triune God.

Although encounters between different traditions may have their initial aim in trying to understand the other tradition better, it is an inevitable side-effect of such encounters that one learns to view one's own tradition from the perspective of the other. This has the effect that views and habits that were hitherto taken for granted within a given tradition are no longer accepted as a matter of course. Now that one has encountered alternatives questions present themselves with regard to views that had so far been unquestioned. It would not be a gross exaggeration to see the mainstream of the history of Western trinitarian reflection as a series of footnotes on Augustine's conception of the Trinity in *De Trinitate*. Augustine's emphasis on the unity of the divine essence of God's triune being, his stress on the undivided mode of God's relating to what is not God and his attempt to trace the intelligibility of the doctrine of the Trinity through the *vestigia trinitatis* in the human consciousness, mediating unity and differentiation, defined the parameters for the mainstream of Western trinitarian reflection. With the encounter with Eastern trinitarianism these presuppositions of Western reflection of the Trinity became the focus of theological attention. The majority of recent studies in trinitarian theology are characterized by a critical attitude towards Augustine's conception of the Trinity. Some attempt to overcome the 'vicissitudes of Western trinitarianism' by seeking orientation in going back behind Augustine to the work of the Cappadocians, others focus on those aspects of Augustine's reflections that had seemed to play a subordinate role in Augustinian trinitarianism, like his use of the model of a relationship of love as the matrix for understanding the trinitarian relations which was later creatively developed by Richard of St Victor. Even those who feel inclined to defend Augustine against these criticism and build constructively on his work now argue for what had been accepted largely without argument. The interplay between the inspiration of Eastern trinitarianism and the self-critical re-examination of the history of Western trinitarianism must certainly be identified as one of the factors leading to the new interest in trinitarian theology.

The effects of the ecumenical encounter with Eastern Orthodoxy are in many ways interconnected with another group of intratheological factors that seem to fuel the new interest in the doctrine of the Trinity. Eastern Orthodoxy's criticism of Western trinitarianism had pointed to a marginalization of the Trinity in Western theological thought. A similar diagnosis was suggested by Karl Rahner who directed theological attention to the structural reasons in the exposition of doctrinal theology that have, in his view, contributed to a situation where the doctrine of the Trinity loses its constitutive role for the argued presentation of the content of Christian faith. If trinitarian reflections follow the argument of the treatise 'De Deo Uno' dealing with the existence and attributes of the one God in a separate treatise 'De Deo Trino' this creates the impression that the statements of the doctrine of the Trinity do not play a constitutive part in reflection on the identity and nature of God. The threeness of God appears merely as a complicating factor of what had been established about the oneness of God, a mystery in danger of clouding what could clearly and distinctly be said about the unity of God. Attempts at recovering the doctrinal significance of the doctrine of the Trinity seem fated to founder unless its displacement in the systematic order of the exposition of Christian doctrines is overcome. Many of the recent attempts at redefining the role of the Trinity in Christian dogmatics have therefore tried to spell out the constructive implications of Rahner's critique of the systematic location of trinitarian discourse in Christian theology. If the understanding of God as Trinity is constitutive for Christian faith it cannot be relegated to the place of a mere appendix of the Christian doctrine of God. Rather, it must be conceived as the gateway through which the theological exposition of all that can be said about God in Christian theology must pass. The doctrine of the Trinity is thus elevated from a place of virtual obscurity to a place of central significance in the systematic structure of Christian dogmatics.

Another related point of Rahner's critique concerns a central point of the internal structure of the doctrine of the Trinity, i.e. the relationship between the immanent and the economic Trinity. Rahner laid his finger on the fact that the conception of the innertrinitarian relations, defined as processions of the Son and the Spirit from the Father were in traditional dogmatics insufficiently related to the missions of the Son and the Spirit expressing the role of the Trinity in the economy of salvation. If these two aspects of trinitarian discourse are separated it follows that the immanent Trinity and the question of the immanent relations in the Godhead become a matter of speculative theology, whereas the economic Trinity is placed in the context of the history of salvation. If discourse about the immanent Trinity and discourse about the economic Trinity are not shown to be constitutively related the history of salvation becomes largely irrelevant for the conception of the triune being of God in its immanent relations, and the trinitarian constitution of God's being becomes irrelevant for the history of salvation. The implications of this separation of the immanent and the economic Trinity are immense. If the divine economy is not conceived as constitutive for gaining knowledge of God's being in its immanent constitution, the issue of the knowability of God becomes paramount, because such a separation would imply that God's revelation could not disclose the divine being in its immanent trinitarian constitution. Conversely, if the immanent constitution of the triune divine being is not actualized in the divine economy, it loses any function for conceiving the relations of God to the world, from the doctrine of creation to the teachings on eschatology. The implications for the method of doctrinal theology are equally far-reaching, because the separation of the immanent and the economic Trinity implies that the scriptural witness to God's relationship with creation in the people of Israel and in Christ is irrelevant for understanding the immanent constitution of the divine being. Speculative theology dealing with the immanent Trinity can thus operate in a territory of its own, unrelated to the work of scriptural exegesis. The principle *sola scriptura* might still be invoked in relation to the divine economy, but there is one area where it does not apply: the immanent trinitarian constitution of the divine being.

Rahner's own solution to these questions was tersely phrased in the statement: 'the immanent Trinity is the economic Trinity, and the economic Trinity is the immanent Trinity'. Since it was first introduced, the discussion of Rahner's axiom for trinitarian theology has continued until today. Explicit agreement with his proposal has come from some quarters, suggestions for qualifications and modifications from others. The focus of the debate continues to be the identity-statement of Rahner's thesis. Is the 'is' of his phrase to be interpreted in the sense of strict identity implying the indiscernibility of identicals, or is some other interpretation of the relationship of immanent and economic Trinity to be preferred? In whatever way this question is answered in different trinitarian theologies, there is almost unanimous agreement that immanent and economic Trinity must be viewed as essentially related. The upshot of this is that biblical exegesis has come back into the debate on trinitarian theology. While there is a consensus that no developed doctrine of the Trinity can be found in the New Testament, there is considerable agreement that the ways in which the relationship of Father, Son and Spirit is depicted in its various forms in the different theologies of the New Testament is relevant, not only for conceiving and interpreting the economic Trinity, but also its relationship to the immanent Trinity.

In addition to the ecumenical encounter between East and West and the intratheological factors just mentioned there is another stimulus at work in the new interest in trinitarian theology. It concerns the relationship between the Christian understanding of God and the view of God in philosophical theism and its critique in modern atheism. It was the challenge of modern atheism, indiscriminately attacking all forms of belief in God, that motivated Christian theologians to question the simple equation between a Christian understanding of God and theism.

Viewed from a historical perspective philosophical theism is closely tied to the historical situation of its origin in the seventeenth century and can be interpreted as the attempt to find a common interpretation of reality in societies torn apart by the religious disputes of the confessional wars. Since the issues that had exercised such a divisive influence on European societies of that period were associated with questions of revealed theology, tied up with historical forms of Christian belief, it seemed plausible to find a common ground for the functioning of the order of society in a form of belief in God which is not based on the historical and therefore always contentious interpretation of Scripture, but which has its ground in human nature as that which is shared by all members of society and can therefore claim authority apart from the claims of religious traditions and communities. In order to pacify confessionally divided societies a clear distinction had to be drawn between those beliefs which were constitutive for the moral consensus of a society and those beliefs which could be held as a personal conviction but could no longer be permitted to define the principle of cohesion of a society. Whereas belief in God, in divine providence, the moral calling of humankind and the immortality of the soul clearly belonged to the first group, specific beliefs about the church, the sacraments and their christological foundations had to be comprised in the second group. For this form of philosophical theism belief in Christ and the experience of salvation in the Christian community could not have a constitutive function for belief in God, thereby excluding precisely those aspects of Christian belief that led to the statement of the doctrine of the Trinity in the early church.

In trying to defend the plausibility of belief in God as the foundation for a consensus concerning fundamental values in society philosophical theists attempted to develop a rational justification of belief in God that could be viewed independently of claims to revelation in history, mediated through the now divided ecclesial communities of interpretation. In this context the arguments of natural theology received new attention and, together with them, those forms of conceiving the divine being, ultimately rooted in Greek metaphysics in its various forms, that had from the outset proved difficult to combine with the Christian experience of salvation in Christ that is the foundation of trinitarian theology.

Can impassibility be seen as a constitutive divine attribute if trinitarian discourse permits and requires the statement that one of the Trinity suffered and died on the cross? Does the God of the Christian Gospel remain transcendent over against the perishing of all worldly being, and if so, can this image of God be reconciled with the view that the summary concept of God is love? Furthermore, a trinitarian understanding of God that understands the immanent and the economic Trinity as related, has to deal with the question how the Son's participation in the time of creation during the Incarnation relates to the understanding of divine eternity. Can the traditional Boethian understanding of divine eternity as timelessness be maintained in a consistently trinitarian conception of God, and if not, how can the doctrine of the Trinity understand the triune God as the creative ground and perfecting end of the time of creation and offer a non-docetic interpretation of the Son's participation in the time of creation?

The attempts at answering such questions differ widely in the various conceptions of trinitarian theology. However, they all seem to agree that the relationship between philosophical theism and Christian trinitarian theology needs to be reexamined. Some would claim that the death of the God of theism heralded by modern atheism signals the advent of an era where the trinitarian understanding of God can be fully appreciated, others see it as dangerous folly to jeopardize the intellectual achievements of theism in the attempt at finding new modes of trinitarian expression in Christian theology. It seems, however, that they all agree in the hope that trinitarian thinking might open new constructive avenues for responding to the different forms of modern atheistic critique of belief in God.

There is a further motive that seems to be connected to the new interest in trinitarian theology. It relates to the fact that our images of God, in one way or another, influence our views of reality by defining attitudes to the natural and the social world that are in accordance with the corresponding image of God. That this is the case is not a matter of theological principle but of historical observation. It is only to be expected if one takes into account that Christian doctrine includes quite a number of 'bridging concepts' relating divine reality to worldly and human reality. The doctrine of creation, expressing the character of the relationship between creator and creature, the doctrine of the *imago Dei*, defining the created destiny of humankind, the doctrine of the Incarnation, depicting the union of divine and human in the person of Christ, the doctrine of the church, developing the metaphors of the people of God or the body of Christ – they all point to ways in which the understanding of God shapes our understanding of the world and our views of who we are. Because of this, knowledge of God and knowledge of ourselves are intrinsically related, and because it includes such 'bridging concepts', doctrinal reflection can have a formative influence on the interpretation and the organization of social reality. The normative character of Christian doctrine includes its formative function for the forms of human community organization.

It is one aspect of recent work in trinitarian theology that it focuses on the different views of human nature, personal identity and social relationships suggested by non-trinitarian and trinitarian conceptions of God. Is there a link between an image of God interpreting God as an individual being conceived on the model of a mind, unrestricted by anything other than itself, and the view of the human being as an individual primarily defined in terms of its rational capacities? Can we trace connections between the image of God as the single supreme ruler, endowed with omniscience and omnipotence, to forms of community organization and social order, characterized by the subordination of the many under a single ruler? What difference would it make if it could be shown that the authentic Christian view of God depicted the triune God as persons in communion relating to one another in a relationship of freedom and love? What difference would it make to forms of community organization in the church and in society if it could be made plausible that the relationship of God to creation is not a relationship of the one over against the many, since in God's being the one and the many are mediated in such a way that both are constitutive for God's trinitarian being?

With regard to such questions doctrinal reflection and the

ideological critique of forms of social order overlap. However, the relationship between our views of God and our views on the order of personal and social relationships is complex. It would be theologically disastrous if one criticized the projection of certain views of the divine nature on the order of human society for its alienating effects, and then proceeded by projecting a view of desirable human relationships on the divine being. Nevertheless, it has to be acknowledged that one of the factors operative in the increased interest in trinitarian theology is an acute awareness of the interrelationship between theological concepts and the conceptions that inform our views of the natural and social world. Theology, we have come to recognize, always has social effects, however indirect they may be. The question that is now on the agenda is whether and to what extent it matters whether our theology is trinitarian or not.

We have tried to indicate some of the factors that have influenced the growth of interest in the doctrine of the Trinity in recent years. Apart from the factors that have been mentioned other factors and motives would have to be investigated in attempting to provide a complete picture of what underlies the increased interest in trinitarian theology. Their significance, however, depends to a large extent on what is seen as the character of trinitarian theology today. It is here that one encounters quite diverse views even among the proponents of trinitarian theology.

It is notoriously difficult to assess the character of contemporary trends and tendencies from the perspective of participant observation – in theology just as in any other sphere of inquiry. Such assessments, so it seems, can more easily be made from a safe historical distance when a school of thought, a theological movement or an intellectual tendency have come to the end of their life-span and can now be assessed as historical phenomena. Yet, one cannot refrain from attempting to assess our own situation if we want to play an active part, however insignificant, in shaping it. What, then, is this new trinitarian orientation in theology? Is it a *revolution* that takes theology into new, hitherto uncharted seas of theological exploration or is it an exercise in *restoration*, recovering the relevance of old truths in a new situation?

Perhaps the best way of interpreting the new interest in trinitarian theology is to see it neither as a revolutionary new departure nor as an exercise in restoration but as a renaissance or as a revival of trinitarian thought. Such a view would not see trinitarian theology as a radically novel way of doing theology, but as an attempt at developing the seminal insights of formative periods in the history of Christian doctrine in order to meet the challenges of a new and in some respects different situation. On this view, trinitarian theology could acknowledge the ambiguity of history in providing the formative conceptualization of a trinitarian understanding of God and in documenting its decline into virtual insignificance in certain phases of the history of doctrine. Interpreting the new interest in trinitarian theology as a renaissance or revival does not imply that today's theological problems could be solved by restoring the teaching of the past in the present. The metaphors of renaissance and revival suggest that there are theological possibilities to be explored which have so far not been explored in the history of doctrine, although these new uses of trinitarian thought are not discontinuous with its past. The measure of continuity and discontinuity cannot be established beforehand; it can only be discovered and established in the context of doing trinitarian theology today.

The conference on 'Trinitarian Theology Today' held in September 1990 by the Research Institute in Systematic Theology at King's College London was intended to take stock of trinitarian theology today and to provide an interim report on its achievements, its problems and its tasks. The papers published in this volume are revised versions of the papers delivered at that conference. The conference organizers had invited Professor Robert W. Jenson to open the conference with what is now fashionably called a 'key-note address' on the question: 'What is the Point of Trinitarian Theology?' In accepting the assignment Professor Jenson immediately introduced an important correction: If theology 'is not initially a second-level discourse' but the 'first-level act of calling on God by the triune name', then 'trinitarian theology does not have a point, it *is* the point' (p. 31). It is the point precisely in the sense that the reply that is evoked in the life of the church by the call of the Gospel 'is an anticipation of the End . . . where we will be initiated into the pattern of God's triune life among the three' (p. 32). Trinitarian theology as this first-level discourse is doxological, because it is eschatological: '[I]f we are now able to shape our liturgy by the processions and glorifications, it is because our minds may trace a logic not yet of this world.' (ibid.) Having established the doxological character of first-level trinitarian discourse Professor Jenson is quick to guard this view against an interpretation that sees this mode of discourse as merely expressive, non-cognitive and subjective. If doxology is indeed a response to the beauty of God, he asks with Jonathan Edwards, is not 'the apprehension of beauty . . . precisely the point where mere "subjectivity" is *overcome*, where our thinking and willing are grasped by reality beyond themselves' (p. 33)?

If trinitarian language is initially situated in the context of doxology, is it possible that it may be translated into another idiom in order to accommodate our modern, and perhaps justified, sensibilities? For Jenson such an attempt must fail, not because the tradition must be maintained at all costs, but because of the intrinsic character of trinitarian discourse. To justify this claim Jenson develops an analogy between the *verba* of trinitarian discourse and the *verba visibilia* of the sacraments which is based on their 'immunity to translation'. In both cases, Jenson argues, we do not know the rules by which these signs are instituted, the rules of their 'home language', and therefore 'we possess no semantic rules . . . for their translation into less offensive terms' (p. 35). The reason for this, in the strict sense pious, agnosticism is that first-level trinitarian discourse is the anticipation of the eschatological doxology. Our partial and anticipatory knowledge of these signs is bound to the historical contingencies of God letting us 'overhear the conversation of heaven' (p. 36) in the story of Israel, Jesus and the church.

Whereas first-level trinitarian discourse, the church's address to God, *is* the point in that it expresses in anticipation the ultimate destiny of humankind, second-level trinitarian discourse in the church's address to the world *has* indeed a point, a specific function. It is 'to maintain against all compunctions that the biblical story about God and us is true of and for God himself' (ibid.). The language of trinitarian doctrine of two unique 'processions' of the Son and the Spirit from the Father so that there 'is a unique relation of each of Father, Son and Spirit to the other two' which establishes the 'triune identity' is for Jenson 'simply the biblical account in drastic summary' (p. 36). It preserves the Gospel's account of God's self-identification as an account of God's own reality. Jenson develops this thesis in two directions: the relationship of God and time, and the question of a narrative causality in God.

When we accept that trinitarian doctrine maintains the truth of the biblical narrative as the truth of God's own reality, then eternity, the mode of God's own reality and, according to Jenson, the ultimate goal of every religious search, cannot be conceived as an absence of time. Trinitarian doctrine preserves the biblical story about God in such a way that the story cannot be transcended in order to find 'the real God'. We therefore have to see the biblical story as a story with three agents, each finding his identity as an agent precisely by distinguishing himself from the other two as God so that in this mutual relationship the identity of each of the three is established. The dynamics of the biblical narrative are, according to Jenson, the concrete content of the tradition's insistence that each of the three is identical with his relationship to the other two. If this relational dynamic is the content of trinitarian discourse, what, then is denoted by 'God'? Jenson's thesis is that ' "God". . . denotes *what happens between* Jesus and the one he calls "Father" and the Father's Spirit in whom Jesus turns to him' (p. 38). Any attempt at defining the divine *ousia* will not be able to go beyond Gregory of Nyssa's answer that it is 'infinity' as such.

How, then, should the relationship of Father, Son and Spirit be seen in connection with the direction of time? For Jenson, the Father is the 'whence' of divine events, the 'Unsent Sender' of the processions of Son and Spirit. The Spirit is the 'whither' of God's life, God as 'the Power of the Future'. If this Power of the Future is to be thought of as active, it follows, Jenson suggests, that there are two 'liberations', of the Father and the Son by the Spirit which complement the two processions from the Father and are equally constitutive of the triune identity and the divine reality. Between the 'whence' and the 'whither' of the Father and the Spirit, between the 'past' and the 'future' there is Jesus Christ as God's 'specious present'. Jenson thus maintains that 'time cannot be extrinsic to God', although he immediately qualifies this by referring to Karl Barth's definition of the eternity of the triune God as '*reine Dauer*', that is 'pure duration', in which the modes of time do not fall apart in that nothing recedes into the past or approaches from the future. Jenson can therefore suggest: 'Time . . . is the *accommodation* God makes in his living and moving eternity, for others than himself.' (p. 40)

This thesis does not simply assert God's temporality over a-
gainst God's eternity, nor is time simply an aspect of God's accommodation to his creatures in the history of salvation which
remains external to God's own reality. The assertion that 'the
biblical story of God and us is true of and for God himself' excludes both possibilities.

The second question Jenson raises also follows from this
central claim of his paper. If the biblical story of God is true for
God himself, does it not follow, that the narrative logic of a
story also applies to God's own reality? The logic of a narrative
is such, as Jenson points out with Aristotle, that events happen in
ways that cannot simply be inferred from antecedent events.
There is genuine novelty and surprise in the course of events, so
that its narrative ordering only becomes transparent from the
outcome of the story. Can this apply to God? Is there narrative
connection in God, a succession of events ordered by their outcome
so that there can be genuine freedom in God's life? For Jenson the
Gospel requires the answer to be affirmative. The specific *locus*
to develop this point is for him the doctrine of the Spirit. It is
the assertion that the Spirit is 'fully one of the Trinity' that enables freedom in God which connects the past and the present
with the future in unexpected ways. 'The Spirit is God as his and
our future rushing upon us, he is the eschatological reality of
God, the Power as which God is the active Goal of all things.'
(p. 41) It is here that, for Jenson, the point of trinitarian theology calls for modifications and new explorations in the traditional forms of explication of trinitarian theology itself.

The second paper, 'The Doctrine of the Holy Trinity: The
Significance of the Cappadocian Contribution', by Professor John
D. Zizioulas has as its theme the legacy of Cappadocian trinitarian thought to trinitarian theology today. Zizioulas points
out that the significance of 'the Cappadocian contribution' goes
beyond dogmatic theology in the narrow sense and has wider implications for European philosophy and culture. He develops the
Cappadocians' seminal insights which have been a major stimulus in the contemporary revival of trinitarian theology by plac-
ing them in their historical context in the debate with Sabellianism and Eunomianism.

The Sabellian interpretation of trinitarian discourse suggesting that 'Father', 'Son' and 'Spirit' are only roles assumed by
the one God in the divine economy raises, Zizioulas explains,

major difficulties for Christian proclamation and worship. Is the testimony of the Gospel of the fully personal reciprocal dialogue of the Son and the Father merely an imaginative elaboration of the relation of the two 'modes' of Father and Son? Whom is the church addressing in praying to the Son, the Father and the Spirit? And if the Father, the Son and the Spirit are merely modes of the appearance of the one God is the divine economy merely a dramatic performance devoid of any 'real' divine involvement? In their attempt at emphasizing the ontological integrity of each person of the Trinity the Cappadocoians rejected the concept of *prosopon* because of its associations with theatrical or social role-playing and inaugurated what Zizioulas calls a 'historic revolution': the identification of the idea of person with that of *hypostasis*.

Is this emphasis on the ontological integrity of Father, Son and Spirit not in danger of developing into tritheism as the imagery of the Cappadocians sometimes seems to suggest, even if they employed the term *ousia* as the general category applicable to more than one person? Zizioulas responds to this question by contrasting the relationship between nature and person in human beings and in the being of God. Whereas in human existence nature precedes person so that a human person is conceived as an individual ontologically independent of other human persons, this is not the case in God. 'Since God by definition has not had a beginning, and space and time do not enter His existence, the three persons of the Trinity do not share a pre-existing or logically prior to them divine nature, but coincide with it. Multiplicity in God does not involve a division of His nature, as happens with man.' (p. 48) The unity in God is not established through participation in a prior common nature, but it is constituted as the unbreakable *koinonia* of the three persons. This is a novel view of the relationship of the 'one' and the 'many': 'The "one" not only does not precede – logically or otherwise – the 'many, but, on the contrary, requires the "many" from the very start in order to exist' (p. 49).

A further development of this innovation was in Zizioulas' view occasioned by the attempt at offering a consistent refutation of Eunomianism, the theory, that, since the divine substance is defined as being unbegotten, only the Father is fully God, whereas the Son, being begotten, is excluded from participation in the divine substance. In response to that the Cappadocians reorganized the rules of predication applying in trinitarian discourse. If the divine substance is unknowable and inexpressible as they believed, any properties (in the sense of identifying descriptions) that can be predicated of God must be predicated of the persons: unbegottenness of the Father, begottenness of the Son and *ekporeusis* of the Spirit. Hypostatic properties are incommunicable and uniquely identify one person, but do so by expressing its relationship to the other two persons. Zizioulas summarizes the ontological implications of this insight in the statement: 'Being is simultaneously relational and hypostatic.' (p. 50)

In developing the philosophical implications of the Cappadocians' view of the Trinity Zizioulas refers to their view of the Father as the *aition*, the 'cause', of divine existence which is designed to interpret the generation of the Son and the *ekporeusis* of the Spirit *not* as the necessary overflow of the divine nature, but as the free personal action of the Father. Consequently, the *monarchia* of God refers, Zizioulas argues, strictly to the person of the Father so that we are confronted with an ontology which gives the person ontological priority over substance. This contains for Zizioulas the main challenge of the Cappadocians' trinitarian thinking to Greek philosophical thought which had in some way always given priority to nature, to the one, over against the plurality of persons. The Cappadocians insisted, according to Zizioulas, that the priority of nature over the person applies only to created existence, but not to the uncreated existence of God in whom the 'one' and the 'many' exist simultaneously because of the ontological primacy of personhood. In making the person of the Father the *aition*, the 'cause', of the Son and the Spirit, they affirmed personal freedom as the 'cause' of being, and this applies in its primary sense to God's own reality: '. . . *what causes God to be is the Person of the Father*, not the one divine substance' (p. 54).

In elaborating the anthropological implications of the Cappadocian doctrine of the Trinity Professor Zizioulas refers again to the distinction between nature and personhood. The destiny of human beings to live as images of God cannot refer to nature, neither to the divine nature which is unknowable nor to the human nature which is bound by the limitations of created existence, it must refer to the calling of human beings to live as images of God's personhood. And this, Zizioulas points out, 'would amount to "becoming God"' (p. 55), the *theosis* of human beings in Greek patristic thought. The call to personhood as the main anthropological implication of the Cappadocian ontology is therefore a call to freedom: '. . . man is called to an effort to free himself from the necessity of his nature and behave in all respects as if the person were free from the laws of nature.' (p. 56) It is here that Professor Zizioulas locates the significance of the ascetic effort the Fathers understood as an essential element of human existence. There are three specific points Professor Zizioulas emphasizes as implications of the Cappadocian ontology of personhood. The first is the special status that is given to the concept of the person. If personhood is 'the "way of being" of God Himself' (ibid.), there is no higher value or necessity to which personhood might be subjected, and in this sense personhood implies radical freedom. The second point concerns the fact that personhood is constituted in relationship and that therefore communion is the mode of personal existence. If communion comes to its fullest actualization in love, then this is where the *logos* of our being resides: 'in the relationship of love that makes us unique and irreplaceable *for another*.' (p. 57) Because it is a relationship that is constituted by and rooted in personhood which has ontological primacy, this relationship can overcome the boundaries and limitations that define our nature. The statement that 'personal identity can emerge only from love as freedom and from freedom as love' (ibid.) therefore applies to God's personal being and to us as far we are images of God as persons. The third point concerns the unique and unrepeatable character of a person. Natures, species and individuals of a species cannot possess or produce a unique identity that does not perish in death. Personal identity is only granted in personal relationship with God's personal and eternal identity.

In his conclusion Professor Zizioulas describes the distinction between nature and person and the suggestion to see identity as defined by the concept of personhood as the one crucial contribution of the Cappadocians' thought to our self-understanding and our understanding of God from which all other aspects follow. The Cappadocians' theology, he contends, is 'basically a soteriological theology', because 'it makes us see in God a kind of existence we all want to lead' (p. 59). The distinction between nature and person also has significant implications for our language of God. If Father, Son and Spirit are the only names of God that signify personal identity they cannot be changed in the attempt at making our language of God more amenable to contemporary concerns. All other language about God can only refer to the nature of God, its qualities or energies which can only be insufficiently known and inadequately expressed. Trinitarian discourse must be the primary way of naming God since it is rooted in participation in the Father-Son relationship through the Spirit as it is revealed in Christ and appropriated in the church. All else, Professor Zizioulas concludes, remains a matter for academic speculation.

Like Professor Zizioulas, Professor John Heywood Thomas approaches in his paper 'Trinity, Logic and Ontology' the theological issues of the doctrine of the Trinity through history. He does so with a specific systematic aim: to clarify 'the logicality of the assertion of the dogma that God is triune' and to discuss 'the coherence of a metaphysic which talks of personal relations within a substantial unity' (p. 61). Approaching these issues through the 'concretions of history' (p. 62) is not only a matter of following the principle that theological and philosophical problems cannot be abstracted from the context of history, but it is rooted in the fact 'that the issue of the Trinity would not arise for us were it not that the faith we discuss is directed towards the God revealed in history' (ibid.). If one inquires into the relationship between logic and the doctrine of the Trinity in this sense one must pay attention to the different senses in which 'logic' is used with regard to different aspects of the doctrine of the Trinity. In his searching and painstaking analysis of the relationship between the doctrine of the Trinity and logic John Heywood Thomas presents a survey of the different ways in which their relationship illuminates the ontological issues of the doctrine of the Trinity.

In order to substantiate his thesis that 'doctrine has . . . been born of logic as Christianity turned the whole world of philosophy upside down' (p. 64) Professor John Heywood Thomas reminds us through various examples of the role logic played in the development of trinitarian theology. In particular he refers to the logical points Anselm elaborated: that there is a difference between properties and relations; that the logic of trinitarian theology is situated in the context of worship; and that the rationality of orthodoxy can be shown by demonstrating the irrationality of its negation. In his discussion of Thomas Aquinas the author refers especially to the starting-point in revelation which, Aquinas argues, is necessary since belief in the Trinity cannot be justified by logical demonstration or by showing the higher degree of probability it has compared to other views of God. The author interprets Aquinas' theology of the Trinity as a revision and correction of Augustine's conception of the Trinity necessitated by the philosophical requirements of Aristotelian metaphysics. This leads to the development of a conceptual map of the doctrine carefully distinguishing processions, relations, persons, notions and missions. John Heywood Thomas illustrates the sophisticated use Thomas made of logic in his differentiation between 'generation' and 'procession' which leads to the proposal of reconstructing trinitarian language in such a way that of the four real relations in God (paternity, filiation, spiration and procession), only three are distinct from one another because of their mutual opposition (the three persons), although they are really identified with the one simple divine essence. This demonstrates for the author that the attempt at understanding God as essentially in relation 'necessitated recourse to the language of ontology' (p. 68).

It is the relationship between logic and ontology which is a recurring theme in the following discussion of the paper. Before turning to this question Professor John Heywood Thomas recapitulates the distinction between sentential logical form and predicate logical form in modern formal logic and demonstrates the ways in which predicate logic is useful in the analysis of trinitarian language, since it clarifies the formal logical differences between different material expressions of doctrine. Although these distinction can be put in precise form with the aid of modern formal logic they were never absent from the debates on trinitarian theology in the history of Christian theology. An example is Calvin's critique of Sabellianism. As Calvin clearly saw, interpreting the statements that the Father is God, the Son is God and the Spirit is God as identity-statements and distinguishing them from predications such as 'God is powerful, wise and just' necessitates, on the presupposition that there is only one God, the assumption of relations in God and so necessitates the introduction of the term 'person' in trinitarian language.

However, once it is established that there are relations in God, how are they to be interpreted? In discussion with Rowan Williams' analysis of Donald MacKinnon's thought the author

maintains that from a logical point of view the relations between the first two persons must be viewed as internal relations
and their assertion must therefore be necessarily true, whereas
the relation of the Father and the Son to the Spirit is an external relation in the logical sense of being irreversible, although it
is not accidental. From a theological point of view this does not
question the statement that there is identity between the three
persons which refers to the one essence, 'a single ontological
nature' (p. 72). The author suggests that this notion of identity
through reference to the unity of essence could perhaps logically
be clarified by employing the notion of functional equivalence
between terms or propositions indicating that they have the
same truth-value in the logical system.

For Professor John Heywood Thomas it must be kept in mind in
all these discussions that '[t]he starting-point of a Trinitarian
theology, then, must be the clarification of what is involved in
[the] confession of Jesus Christ as Lord' (p. 73f). It is the 'indissoluble relation of God and Christ' (p. 74) that forms the basis of
trinitarian discourse. If both statements about relation in God
and statements about the unity of God seem theologically
necessary in view of God's revelation in Christ, could it not be,
Professor Heywood Thomas asks, that much of the opposition to
Trinitarianism can be traced back to semantic confusions about
basic trinitarian concepts such as 'relations' and 'properties'? He
suggests to distinguish sharply between the *fact* that the
Father, like the Son and the Spirit, is a member of the group of
three and the *relation* of the Father to the group. In this sense
'we can distinguish the relation the Father, Son and the Spirit
independently have to the Trinity from the property of having
this relation which belongs to all three' (p. 77).

The point of this attempt to spell out the ontological implications of logical distinctions in trinitarian language is 'finding
ways of talking of the reality of the three Persons of the Trinity'
(p. 77). It is required and supported by 'the reality of Christian
experience from which the postulate of a Trinity is made'
(ibid.). It is the 'completeness of the victory' of Christ on the
cross and the 'completeness of the fulfilled promise' (p. 78) in the
story of the young church which necessitated the trinitarian
scheme emphasizing both the reality of the persons of the Trinity and the unity of the divine essence. It is this experience and
the hope that death is transcended with all its ontological implications that lies at the root of trinitarian faith.

The next two papers by Dr Brian Horne and Professor Colin Gunton focus on the relationship of trinitarian theology to art and the sciences respectively and so direct our attention to the relevance of trinitarian thought to our engagement with reality in its different forms. In his paper 'Art: A Trinitarian Imperative?' Brian Horne begins with Michael Tippett's view that the faculty to create is 'a true fundamental . . . part of what we mean by having knowledge of God' (cf. p. 80). Although since the Enlightenment the general tendency of aesthetic theory has been shaped by the emphasis on the autonomy of art over against religion, Dr. Horne refers two recent thinkers, who would, on the basis of aesthetic considerations, argue for taking seriously the view expressed by Michael Tippett. One is the art critic Peter Fuller who, although he calls himself 'an incorrigibile atheist', argues that in the situation of the 'ever-present absence of God' aesthetic experience provides 'the sole remaining glimmer of transcendence', the hope for 'redemption through form' (cf. p. 81). In the context of his programmatic attempt at recovering the spiritual in art Fuller refers to an essay by P. T. Forsyth where he states that '. . . [o]ne way of thinking about God makes Art impossible, another makes it inevitable'. This notion of the inevitability of art provides the main focus for Dr Horne's essay. Is the inevitability of art to be explained as the necessary illusion that makes the absence of meaning bearable? Or is any meaning art may provide, as Theodor W. Adorno seems to suggest, so enclosed in its aesthetic form that its relation to reality outside the work of art is rendered wholly problematical?

The second thinker Brian Horne refers to is George Steiner who also sees art as inevitable in human culture, as necessary for humans to be human. As in Peter Fuller's work the ascription of meaning requires for Steiner the use of theological categories: 'The meaning of meaning is a transcendent postulate.' (cf. p. 84) The necessity of creating form is for Steiner ultimately rooted in that we have been created form. Dr Horne traces this motif back to the classical Western Catholic tradition where the possibility of human creation is interpreted as grounded in the fact that humans are created in the image of God. If human creativity has its source in that humans are made in the image of the creator, artistic creativity is not a decorative ornament of human existence, but belongs to the essence of what it means to be human.

The necessity of art, however, is different from other necessities of life, like the provision of the means of survival. Although its has the appearance of gratuitousness, it is the field where humans express their humanity in a radical and unique freedom. George Steiner interprets this freedom as absolute freedom, as the power not to create. It is at this point, Dr Horne argues, that the theologian must contradict: 'God alone possesses absolute freedom ... His creature, on the other hand, the human being, by contrast and logical definition possesses only relative freedom and is subject to the necessity of creation.' (p. 86) Dr Horne argues that the paradox of Fuller's and Steiner's position, arguing for a transcendent horizon of artistic creativity and yet denying the reality of God, can be overcome when we turn from a monotheistic or unitarian concept of God as undifferentiated Being to a trinitarian understanding of God. A trinitarian concept of God is the presupposition for achieving what their aesthetic theories seek: 'the reconciliation of transcendence and immanence' (p. 86).

For Brian Horne the human creative drive to externalize bears witness to the fact that human beings are created in the image of the triune God. 'The image in which we are created and understand ourselves refers back to a life in which there is the external self-expression of the Father in his Son or Word and the eternal self-knowledge received in the flowing out and returning of the Spirit.' (p. 87) We may follow Steiner in believing that there is art because there is creation. However, if creation is the work of the triune God it must not be conceived as 'counter-creation', the protest of the human maker against the transcendent creator. At the root of this notion lies the 'unwillingness to recognize the possibility of the divine mystery as (I use Steiner's word) radically immanent, the Holy Spirit, as well as ultimately transcendent, the Father, and the union of these two modes of Being in the expressive form of the Incarnate Son, that projects this formulation of the artistic creation as counter-creation' (p. 88).

Steiner's aim of finding 'real presence' can only be achieved on the basis of a trinitarian view of God locating the possibility of artistic creation in the doctrine of the image (creation), its propriety in the doctrine of the Incarnation and its inevitability in the doctrine of the Holy Spirit enabling 'the human artwork

. . . to become the expressive form of divine radiance' by 'the human will responding freely to the movement of the Holy Spirit' (p. 90). It is the trinitarian view of God which is the foundation for understanding the inevitability of art: 'Since self-expressive energy has been revealed to us as the very structure of the life of God, it cannot be an activity which is optional in the life of creatures who are made in that image: it is a Trinitarian imperative. We may not choose *not* to create if we are to be human.' (p. 92)

In his paper 'Relation and Relativity: The Trinity and the Created World' Professor Colin Gunton begins with a consideration of the relationship between words and the world. On the basis of a discussion of the strength and weaknesses of the two most influential models for conceiving this relationship, Plato's 'realistic idealism' and Kant's 'subjective idealism', Colin Gunton suggests 'that the transcendentals emerge in the interaction between mind and world' (p. 95). This raises the 'question of whether things make themselves known to us in such a way that our concepts are . . . a response to something prevenient' (ibid.). The theological question appears when we inquire about the 'whence' of this prevenience and of the capacity of response. The central objective of Professor Gunton's paper can be expressed in the question, 'whether concepts generated by theology, and particularly trinitarian theology, bear any relation to those employed in conceiving the world as it is presented to us in some of the discoveries of modern science' (p. 96). Professor Gunton makes clear that such an inquiry does not presuppose that the being of the world is in the image of God – that remains the privilege of persons. His inquiry is, rather, concerned with 'conceptual parallels between the concepts in which the being of God is expressed and the ways in which we may conceive the world' (p. 97).

As the background of such an inquiry Colin Gunton presents the main outlines of a trinitarian theology of creation. Its focus is 'the relation-in-otherness between God and the world that is conceived with the help of the doctrine of the Trinity' (p. 98) which allows us to understand the world, because it is created through the Son, as good and destined for redemption and even as already participating in it through the activity of the Spirit, and yet see creation as a free act of God's love. There are three trinitarian concepts which seem to point to conceptual parallels between theology and recent scientific thought. The first is the concept of relation, developed to express the way in which the three persons of the Trinity are to each other in a mutual relationship of love. Since these relations are constitutive for the being of God, 'God's being is a being in relation, without remainder relational' (p. 99). The second concept is that of freedom which is entailed in the understanding of the relations in the Trinity as a relationship of love. Professor Gunton argues that since freedom is found in the obedience of Jesus as the Son to the Father which is enabled by the Spirit we may theologically assume a corresponding freedom in the relations of the eternal Trinity. In this way he develops an analogy of freedom based on the idea that freedom 'is a function of relations between persons and between persons and their world' (p. 100). Can this concept be relevant for our understanding of the non-personal world? The third concept is that of the divine energies, developed to characterize divine activity towards creation but, as Colin Gunton argues, also indicating an inner dynamic in God's relational being if the dynamics of God's relationship to creation derive from the dynamic of God's being.

After illustrating the oscillation between a static and a dynamic view of the universe in the history of Christian thought, Professor Gunton examines the relationship of the three trinitarian concepts of freedom, relation and energy to modern scientific thought. It is the first of these concepts, freedom, which raises the most serious problems since it cannot be directly translated from the personal to the non-personal realm. In moving from the personal to the non-personal realm, Colin Gunton argues, the concept of freedom is transmuted into that of contingence. He then surveys the different aspects in which the concepts of contingence, relation and energy are employed in recent scientific theories and carefully notes the similarities and dissimilarities that appear between the scientific and the theological use of such concepts. What emerges is a surprising correspondence between the rejection of a necessitarian, substantialist and static understanding of the reality of the world in science and of the reality of God in trinitarian theology. However, their difference and relationship comes to its clearest expression in the contrast of an immanent scientific eschatology and a trinitarian theological eschatology, although Professor Gunton emphasizes that the latter is realized within the dynamics of the former. These findings lead him to call for a different way of conducting the dialogue between theology and the sciences 'by means of a comparison and contrast of overlapping concepts' (p. 109).

There are two conclusions Professor Gunton draws from this investigation of the conceptual interface between trinitarian theology and the sciences. The first is that the inquiry into the nature of the world we live in is not merely a matter of dialogue between science and theology. In this dialogue ultimate questions appear which point to the intrinsic connection between ontology and ethics. The second point is that if the dialogue between theology and the sciences points to the discovery of valid relations between words and the world we have found a means of overcoming the cultural fragmentation which threatens in the modern world. The renewal of a common language, Professor Gunton argues, is 'the precondition for the renewal of social order' (p. 110). A trinitarian doctrine of creation is for Colin Gunton 'a prime desideratum for modern Christian theology' (p. 111) because it is the place where the relation between words and the world is approached from the wider perspective of the relation of the triune God to creation.

The last two papers in this collection investigate the relationship of trinitarian theology to two central doctrines of Christian theology, i.e. Christology and eschatology. In his paper 'Christology and Trinitarian Thought' Professor Christoph Schwöbel describes the state of Christology in the modern era as one of crisis. The crucial symptoms of this state of crises he sees in three antinomies which have dominated christological reflection since the Enlightenment: the antinomy between 'the historical' and 'the ultimate', between past and present and the antinomy between being and meaning. Christology today, Schwöbel contends, presents us with a picture of disintegration: 'Modern Christology seems to be increasingly unable to conceive and to conceptualize the unity of the person of Christ and seems to be left with the fragments of the 'historical Jesus', the 'Christ of faith' and the 'Son of God' of christological dogma.' (p. 119)

After surveying the symptoms of the ills of modern Christology the author suggests as a diagnosis that the present state of crisis is 'due to the neglect of the trinitarian logic of the Christian understanding of God and its implications for the

Christian understanding of what it means to be human' (p. 119).
In order to delineate the fundamental strands of the trinitarian
logic of faith he attempts to identify the roots of trinitarian
teaching in the different models, metaphors and paradigms
employed by the different theologies of the Old and New
Testaments. He claims 'that we detect in the expressions of
Christian practice in worship, proclamation, reflection and
action an underlying *proto-trinitarian depth structure* which
provides the focus for the identity of the Christian message and
defines the framework for the pluriformity of the rich variety of
expressions of Christian faith' (p. 126). It provided the basis for
the conceptual expression of the trinitarian logic of Christian
discourse in the interaction between the Christianization of
Hellenism and the Hellenization of Christianity.

The third section of the paper recounts the crucial steps in the
development of the doctrine of the Trinity in its relation to
Christology, from Irenaeus to the Cappadocian Fathers and to
the Council of Chalcedon. Schwöbel sees a difference between
the development of trinitarian doctrine where the Cappadocians 'turned the criticism of inadequate conceptions . . . into a
constructive proposal' and the development of Christology
'where criteria were asserted which could exclude inadequate
conceptions but did not directly suggest a constructive solution' (p.
133). In connection with the increasing marginalization of the
doctrine of the Trinity in Western theology after Augustine this
had the long-term effect of making christological problems
'almost intractable, a formidable challenge for logicians and
metaphysicians and a breeding-ground for paradox' (p. 136) – a
situation which already contains the elements of the modern
state of crisis in Christology.

Against this backdrop Schwöbel turns from diagnosis to
therapy by inviting 'careful consideration of tentative proposals
which might indicate possibilities of overcoming the present
state of crisis' (p. 137). Developing a trinitarian hermeneutic for
Christology requires, first of all, relocating Christology in the
life of the Christian community whose existence is part of the
divine economy. Secondly, this task implies a 'paradigm shift
from natures to persons, from substance metaphysics to a metaphysics of relations' (p. 140), locating the divinity of Christ not
in the possession of a divine nature but in the relation of Sonship
to the Father mediated in the Spirit, and interpreting the hu-

manity of Christ as the reconstitution of true humanity 'the fulfilment of the relational existence of human being in dependence on the triune God' (p. 141). Thirdly, this proposal leads to a new conception of the *enhypostasia* of the humanity of Christ in the person of the Son, describing the identity of Christ the incarnate Son in terms of his being in two relationships, the trinitarian relations of Father, Son and Spirit and the relational existence of humanity. This conceptuality of two 'sets of relationships' is suggested as an alternative to the conceptual scheme of two natures which can also satisfy the criteria of the Chalcedonian Definition. The paper concludes with reflections on how a trinitarian hermeneutic for Christology could help to overcome the antinomies described as the symptoms of the crisis of Christology at the beginning of the discussion.

The last paper in this collections deals, not inappropriately, with eschatology, the doctrine of the Last Things. In his essay 'The Eschatological Roots of the Doctrine of the Trinity' Professor Ingolf Dalferth relates two prominent features of twentieth century theology: the 'recovery of the eschatological dimension' and the 'renaissance of the doctrine of the Trinity' (p. 146). For Dalferth this is not a mere coincidence but points to a central aspect of Christian theology which he presents as the main thesis of his paper: ' [O]nly a trinitarian account of God is true to the foundational experience of the Christian faith: the experience of the eschatological reality of the risen Christ.' (ibid.) In order to offer reasons why this should be so Professor Dalferth, first of all, provides a survey of the main conceptions of trinitarian theology in contemporary German Protestant theology. One of the main features of the trinitarian theologies he discusses is their anti-theism, the rejection of the philosophical theism developed in the Enlightenment, and the attempt at transcending the alternative between theism and atheism. Professor Dalferth's critical discussion of the trinitarian theologies of Eberhard Jüngel, Jürgen Moltmann, Wolfhart Pannenberg and Falk Wagner uncovers another common motif in contemporary trinitarianism: its christological orientation (cf. p. 155). In Dalferth's interpretation this is not only true of Jüngel and Moltmann, who present the theology of the cross and the Trinity as intrinsically related. It also applies to Pannenberg's account of the self-differentiation of Jesus from the Father as the access to our understanding of the trinitarian relations and to Wagner who claims that the Christian understanding of God, rooted in the cross and resurrection of Christ, can be rationally demonstrated as a universal truth about God. The two motifs that shape the renewed interest in trinitarian theology, Dalferth argues, are neither unrelated nor are they truly foundational. He suggests 'that both the anti-theism and the christological orientation of trinitarian theology today are due to, and are a by-product of, the eschatological re-orientation of theology in our century' (p. 155).

According to Dalferth this eschatological re-orientation is the result of a complex development reflected in the shifts of meaning the term eschatology underwent. Its main stages he neatly summarizes in the formula: 'From the *eschata* to the *eschaton*, and from the *eschaton* to the *eschatos*.' (p. 157) The traditional doctrine of the Last Things is thus transmuted into an existential theory of the ultimate meaning of historical being and then transformed into the explication of 'the one eschatological reality of the risen Christ' (p. 158).

In the third section of his paper Professor Dalferth attempts to show how the eschatological nature of Jesus' life, death and resurrection which is disclosed to us as we are 'drawn into the salvific presence of God's love by the power of the Spirit' (p. 159) calls for a trinitarian account of God. There are three constitutive aspects of the eschatological reality to which Christian theology refers which determine the trinitarian explication of the Christian understanding of God. It is *divinely constituted* and so reflects the absolute creativity of God the Father; it is *christologically determined* which expresses the disclosure of God's relationship with us as one of unrestricted and inexhaustible love in Jesus Christ; and it is experienced as the *radical break-through of a new life* which has its ground in the activity of the eschatological Spirit. The doctrine of the Trinity can be called the 'summary grammar' of the Christian account of God since it relates the discourse of faith to the eschatological reality of the risen Christ. Moreover, the distinction and relation of Father, Son and Spirit offers an 'integrating pattern for all aspects of Christian life, experience, thought and action' (p. 166). As such, Professor Dalferth concludes, the doctrine of the Trinity 'is not a speculative theory about the inner life of God but a practical doctrine' (p. 168). Over against all other theoretical external perspectives on God it seeks to remain true to the practi-

cal internal perspective of believers by expressing the constitutive elements of salvific knowledge in its account of 'God as
Father (God's initiative), Spirit (God's direct co-presence with
us) and Son (God's intelligible mediation)' (p. 168). In this way,
Dalferth states, the doctrine of the Trinity has a regulative
function in that it insists on difference between our conceptions of
God and the reality of God and directs us to the eschatological
reality of Christ as the ultimate and therefore paradigmatic
self-communication of God's love.

The papers published in this volume present not only the
present state of trinitarian theology in its various forms of expression and the problems it faces. They also point to the tasks
trinitarian thinking is confronted with. This indicates that trinitarian theology today is not a finished programme of theological thought, but theological reflection on the way – and thus
it reflects the unfinished and provisional character of the
theologia viatorum.

1. What is the Point of Trinitarian Theology?

Robert W. Jenson

I.

I do not remember who suggested the title of this essay. Whoever did it, I do not repent the decision and do intend to stick to the assignment. Yet everything I might say in response to this question would be misleading if I did not first enter and indeed elaborate a disclaimer.

'Theology' is not *initially* a second-level discourse. Thus 'trinitarian theology' is not initially the sort of reflective enterprise which appears in such works as my own; initially it is rather the first-level act of calling on God by the triune name, and of making prayers and sacrifices that follow the triune logic and use the triune rhetoric. And in this mode, trinitarian theology does not have a point, it *is* the point.

The chief end of the human creature is – it may be permissible in this venue to say – to enjoy and glorify God forever. In the communal life of the church we are permitted to anticipate that eternal destiny. And that we may call on God as 'Father, Son and Spirit', that we may direct the attention of our prayers and sacrifices by icons and rhetoric which evoke the great One-in-Three, that we may weave the structure of our liturgy by the logic of the missions and processions, this *is* that anticipation.

You have invited a representative of an in Britain now exotic species of Christian: I am a Lutheran. And I must not disappoint the legitimate expectations attached to such an invitation. So I will bring my reflection under way by saying the Lutheran thing: the 'true treasure' and singular occupation of the church is the holy gospel of our Lord Jesus Christ, that is, the true treasure of the church is the message that one, this one, Jesus the Son of David, the strange rabbi, healer and prophet from Nazareth, is risen from the dead, so as to live and reign for all eternity. The whole life of the church is therefore a great discourse, a great communal talking, about this Jesus and about his resurrection and his coming.

There is, however, an obvious point to do with this discourse of which we Lutherans are, surprisingly, not always so adept: in that the holy gospel is indeed a *gospel*, a word addressed straight to the sheer existence of its hearers, it solicits reply. The reply, moreover, is to *God*, for – and here I may again happily exploit my Lutheranism – the gospel, precisely as a message brought by human speakers, is God's own utterance, the word of God in the simplest sense. Indeed, 'solicits' and 'reply' are far too weak: the gospel does not itself occur apart from the response of prayer and praise and sacrifice. Thus the 'discourse' that is the life of the church is yet better evoked as a great '*conversation*', a conversation between God and humanity.

Conveniently, therefore, the life of the church may be – for purposes of analysis only – considered under two great directorial rubrics: we may think of the church insofar as it speaks *for* God to his creatures, and we may think of the church as it speaks *to* God. As the church labours to speak for God, i.e., to speak the gospel, trinitarian theology indeed *has* a function; and I will make much of it. But, over against my assignment, I must first evoke the life of the church as address *to* God; and this life and address simply *is* an anticipation of the End, in which trinitarian discourse is the point and does not merely have one.

All our trinitarian talk may, of course, be illusion. But if God's true name actually is 'Father, Son and Spirit', then the sounding of this name is a distinctive event of what is to happen around the throne; and when we now and here dare sound it, we claim place in that gathering. If indeed God may be seen in such great visions as of the throne and the lamb or of the fires, it is only the saints whose eyes are transformed to such vision, and the seers permitted momentarily to join them behind the veil of the future; our icons and rhetoric must therefore either be misrepresentations or be *mimesis* guided by their sight rather than our own. It is throughout eternity that we will be initiated into the pattern of God's triune life among the three; if we are now able to shape our liturgy by the processions and glorifications, it is because our minds may trace a logic not yet of this world.

There are two somewhat more prosaic points I want to make about trinitarian speech to God. I can take time only to present them, hardly to argue them.

I. A.

The first: the 'doxological' character of central trinitarian sentences has routinely been noted. Such a sentence as 'The Son is begotten by the Father' is not in the first instance a theoretical proposition *about* two entities so designated; its primary form is 'Oh, Christ our Lord, only Begotten of the Father', spoken in the face of the one so described. It is in the first instance precisely praise, direct personal compliment.

So far, perhaps, so good. But this linguistic observation is sometimes used to suggest that trinitarian discourse, just insofar as it is doxological, does not function cognitively, so that, for example, a sentence like 'The Son is begotten by the Father' should not be used as a premise in deductive reasoning. Praise is a mode of *aesthetic* response; the doxological character of the church's liturgy is response to God's *beauty*; and 'Beauty', we moderns all do think even if we are trained to shy from the banality, 'is in the eye of the beholder'.

But even within the restraints and opportunities of modernist reflection there is a quite opposite possibility. A hero of mine, a notable Enlightener, and the one whom I take to be the greatest English-writing theologian ever, Jonathan Edwards, made it the epistemological hinge of this thought, that the apprehension of beauty is precisely the point where mere 'subjectivity' is *overcome*, where our thinking and willing are grasped by reality beyond themselves. According to Edwards, the apprehension of beauty is the very event in which our thinking and willing are first founded as successful intentions of an other.[1]

Western thought's characteristic dialectic of the good, the true and the beautiful is unavoidably a trinitarian dialectic. In my judgment, this characteristic of our thinking is a blessed theological opportunity, even if the original identifications were a creative misunderstanding. I wish to affirm also the perhaps mostly implicit correlation of the Spirit, as the glorifier of the Father and the Son, with beauty. I will even surmise that it has been Western trinitarianism's inadequate

---

[1] Cf. Robert W. Jenson, *America's Theologian. A Recommendation of Jonathan Edwards*, New York/Oxford: Oxford University Press 1988, pp. 15–49.

understanding of the Spirit[2] that is behind our worry that beauty is merely 'subjective'. Be that as it may, Edwards' freedom from that worry was enabled precisely by the vigour with which he affirmed the doctrine that God *is* Spirit, and with which he identified the specific act of the Spirit in the events of creation and sanctification.

The Spirit, Edwards said, plays the same role in the life of the elect that he does in God's own life, and it is just *so* that their knowledge and will are established beyond themselves in God. Both in God's life and ours, he said, the Spirit *illumines*, and thus founds, what he called the 'sense of the heart'. This 'sense' is the apprehension of beauty and therefore is the transcendental unity of the person.[3]

I. B.

The second: much of the church is now tormented by the campaign of gnostic feminists to replace the triune name with formulations that avoid 'Father' and 'Son'. Some of us are sure that all such translations are just as such profoundly wrong, that they must indeed in churchly practice amount to simple apostasy, and that this would be true even if replacement formulas were found which, unlike the common 'Creator, Redeemer and Sanctifier', avoided modalism.

Now, I do have arguments to that effect, and with the most careful and continuous self-critique I can summon remain convinced of their validity. And yet I am aware that these arguments are after the fact, that I was sure of the position before I discovered them and would remain sure of the position if they were discredited. This may, of course, show that I am immune to reason. But in preparation for this occasion, it ocurred to me to give myself the benefit of a doubt, and examine the intuition itself, for its content and possible basis.

Trinitarian praise is anticipation of utterance around the throne. I suggest that therefore the triune name, and the triune visions and the triune logic, share certain characteristics of those more-than-linguistic signs we in the West call 'sacra-

---

[2] To which see, provisionally, Robert W. Jenson, *Unbaptized God. The Basic Flaw in Ecumenical Theology*, Minneapolis: Fortress Press 1992, pp. 132–47.
[3] Cf. Jenson, *Unbaptized God*, pp. 65–78.

ments', most notably in this context their immunity to translation. It is, I suggest, an intuition of the sheer sacrament-like weight and density of the signs themselves – of the sheer token-types 'Father, Son and Holy Spirit', or 'begotten, not made', or 'proceeding' – that restrains some of us from acceding to proposals for their translation into less offensive terms.

We are not in position to create a ceremony of initiation – say, the giving of a particular life-long haircut – and declare that this will now mean what baptism has meant, because we possess no semantic rules by which the translation could be controlled. The bath may indeed be minimal or maximal, in running water or a basin, done with great ceremonial or great simplicity, but Christian initiation will be accomplished by a bath or not at all.

Every sign, of course, is something before it has a meaning; in Augustinian language, it is a *'res'* before it is a *'signum'*. So a loaf of bread or a hand on the head or a dash of water are all somethings. But an articulated sound or inscribed mark or regulated hand-gesture that belongs to a *language*, can be replaced in the language by some other sound or mark or gesture, following the semantic rules that articulate the language's working. The Supper's loaf or baptism's bath cannot be replaced, because we do not know the rules by which they were instituted. We know that they are signs, and can even take them as signs into our discourse, with *its* rules. Indeed, after the fact we can even work out how these signs are apt to their purpose, why for example bread and cup are apt to mean the crucified Messiah. But we do not know the rules of these signs' home language; we do not know why God says 'I am with you' by bread and cup *instead* of by some other signs. For us, this is simply an historical contingency, to which we are bound as we are bound to the contingencies of God's choice of Israel and of Mary from the maidens of Israel and of Jesus from her many possible children. And so we are not able to translate bread and cup into true equivalents; the types themselves are inseparable from their meaning.

The language by whose rules bread and cup or bath – or the cross-sign or any others of the church's distinctive signs – are instituted, is the language of God and his saints.[4] It is the language

[4] Thomas Aquinas, *Summa Theologiae*, I, 1, 2: *scientia Dei et beatorum*. To this eschatological character of theology according to Thomas, see Robert W. Jenson, *The Knowledge of Things Hoped For*, New York: Oxford University Press 1969, pp. 58–98.

of a community to which we now belong only across the line of our own death and new creation. Thus our possession now of some of its signs is *mysterious* in the strictest sense. For it is identical with the identity across death and resurrection of the sinners that were with the saints that will be.

And the same – I suggest – is true of the dense signs of trinitarian praise. The saints in heaven may know God so well as to make new names for him to suit their love, perhaps they do it instant by instant; but we have membership in their company only across death and resurrection. How do we know what God's name is? Only if he lets us overhear the conversation of heaven, across the border of our own non-being and new being. And *why* he and his saints let us overhear one name instead of another we may think equally suited, we do not know at all.

It is not so that we have a denotative grasp on God, and thereupon coin a name to bring it to speech. We are given the name, and learn from it who and where and when God is. It is not so that we first inhabit God's life, and thus know to construct such sentences as 'the Son proceeds from the Father'; we overhear such things said, and precisely and only so inhabit God's life.

II.

I am, at last, finished with the preliminary warning, and may safely turn to the church's address to the world, and to the function which trinitarian theology indeed 'has' in it. That function, I suggest, is to maintain against all compunctions that the biblical story about God and us is true of and for God himself.

To rehearse classic doctrine:[5] there are in God two incommensurable 'processions', of the Son and the Spirit, from the Father; therefore there is a unique relation of each of Father, Son and Spirit to the other two; and finally therefore there are truly three in God. But these 'processions' are simply the biblical account in drastic summary, construed as an account of God's own reality.

Already the caution of my immediately previous formulations shows what compunctions trinitarian teaching

---

[5] For my understanding of trinitarian doctrine generally, Robert W. Jenson, *The Triune Identity*, Philadelphia: Fortress Press 1982. The following partly summarizes this work, and partly hopes to improve it.

combats, and how strong they are. It was the great single dogma
of late Mediterranean antiquity's religion and irreligion, that no
story can be 'really' true of God, that deity equals 'impassibility'. It is not merely that the gospel tells a story about the
object of worship; every religion of antiquity did that. The gospel *identifies* God as 'He who brought Israel from Egypt and our
Lord Jesus from the dead'. Therefore the gospel cannot rescind
from its story at any depth whatsoever of experience, mystical
penetration or *theologia*. Developed trinitarian liturgy and
theology appeared as the church maintained the gospel's identification of God in the very teeth of what everybody knew to be
of course and obviously true of God, and in every nook of practice
or theory where uncircumcised theological self-evidency lurked.

The function of trinitarian theology is to maintain against all
compunctions that the biblical story of God and us is true of and
for God himself. There are two lines on which I will further ana-
lyse this function.

II. A.

The first: if a story is to be true of God's own reality, then God's
eternity cannot be the simple absence of time. Then God's eternity must be for him something like what time is for us.

Religion – if I may here venture a drastically simplifying description of this multiple and ambiguous phenomenon – is the cul-
tivation of eternity. I venture to say so much precisely, of course,
because I thereby say so very little. For the word 'eternity' by itself is a mere place-marker: it only denotes whatever it is on
which a particular spiritual community relies to join the poles of
time, to knit future and past into a coherent fabric.

The substance of every human act is the particular way it
rhymes remembrance and anticipation into lived present meaning. Just so every human act assumes that the threads of time can
indeed be knit together, that the discontinuities of temporal existence are *somehow* bracketed – that Sartre was wrong.

Every human act relies on some eternity or other. But there
are thus as many putative eternities as there are religions – or
better vice versa. Putative eternities range from the abstract
timelessness of the turning wheel's still centre to the contin-
gency-conquering experience of the great ancestors. The question –
or anyway a big question – about any putative God is: *How*

exactly is this candidate eternal? And not every possible eternity is the mere negation of time, as is shown by the case of the ancestors.

There are three in God in that (1) the Bible tells precisely a story about God; in that (2) it tells its story in such fashion that we cannot transcend the story in some way to find the 'real' God, without declaring the story to be merely false; in that (3) this story about God presents us with three agents of its action; and in that (4) within the story each of the three acts as divine agent precisely by referring to one of the other two as God and distinguishing himself from that other. The first two of these points were fully clear to me when I wrote *The Triune Identity*, the second two were much clarified for me by Wolfhart Pannenberg's work.[6]

The last of the four points must be made a touch more concrete. Christ refers all homage from himself to the one who 'sent' him, to his 'Father', just so accomplishing our salvation and appearing as the Son. This God is the Father only as the one so addressed by the Son; and he then appears in the story centrally as he turns over divine rule to the Son and indeed at the cross 'abandons' his role as God, leaving the Son to suffer the consequences of godhead by himself. And the Spirit glorifies as God and testifies to as God the Father or the Son, exactly so enabling the proposition 'God *is* Spirit'.

Thus it can be said, as the tradition has consistently done, that each of the three is identical with his relation to the other two. And it can further be said, as the tradition has not quite so consistently done, that 'God' simply as such denotes *what happens between* Jesus and the one he calls 'Father' and the Father's Spirit in whom Jesus turns to him. 'God' simply as such denotes the Father's sending and the Son's obedience, the Spirit's coming to the Son and the Son's thanksgiving therefore to the Father – and so on in a dialectic to which only failing insight or imagination sets limits. 'God', simply as such, denotes a life, as the Eastern tradition has put it, a complex of *'energeia'*.

If there is, as traditionally has been taught, such a thing as a sheer divine *'ousia'*, a sheer deity, then this is what Gregory of Nyssa said it is, 'infinity' merely as such. If we ask what it is

---

[6] See now Wolfhart Pannenberg, *Systematische Theologie*, vol. I, Göttingen: Vandenhoeck & Ruprecht 1988, pp. 283–364.

that is infinite, so as thereby to be God, we return to the life among Father, Son and Spirit. We may even venture to say: it is the action of the story told by the Bible that is the referent of 'God', in that this story is encompassing, in that it brackets time.

Finally in this part, I must note the connection between the directions of time and the mutual roles played by Father, Son and Spirit in the biblical story of God. I will abstract and schematize drastically.

The Father appears always as the 'whence' of divine events, as the Given from which they come or to which they return. In classical formulations, the biblical God-story is summarized in the two 'sendings', of the Son and the Spirit; the Father is the Unsent Sender. And as this story asserted to be true of and in God himself, by the doctrine of 'processions' correlated to the 'sendings', classical formulations summarize the relational life of God again in but two processions of the Son and the Spirit from the Father, who has himself no procession.

Correspondingly, the Spirit appears as the 'whither' of God's life. Throughout the biblical story, the Spirit is God as, to accept an inevitable cliché, 'the Power of the future'. The Spirit is God coming from the future to break the present open to himself. The Spirit is divine self-transcendence, insofar as God does not depend upon what is not God to be the referent or energy of his coming to himself. The 'whither' of divine events is not their passive aiming point, but their agent in this mode.

It cannot be said that this biblical identity of the Spirit comes very freely to expression in classical technical formulations, at least in the West. Indeed, one aspect of this lack has been a reproach of Orthodoxy against the West for centuries; and its more general repair is a main project of the current revival of trinitarian speculation. Indeed, I must here project a small effort of the sort, to which I will also recur in the next section. We must, it seems to me, learn to say something along these lines: as there are two sendings/processions of/in God, so there are two – perhaps the word is suitable – *liberations*, of the Father and the Son by the Spirit. And these liberations are as constitutive of the identity and reality of God as are the processions.

Finally, we may perhaps say that the Son is God as his own 'specious present'. It is Jesus the Christ in whom the Father finds himself; and it is Jesus the Christ whom the Spirit liberates from sinking into the past, in whose resurrection the Spirit's liberating act is powerful.

In his treatise on God's eternity, Karl Barth defined the particular 'eternity of the *triune* God' as '*reine Dauer*', as a 'duration', but a duration that is not a struggle. And it may be that Barth has said what there is to say on that topic: 'That being is eternal, in whose duration beginning, succession and end . . . do not fall apart . . .' 'That between source, movement and goal there is no conflict but only peace . . ., distinguishes eternity from time. They are not, however, distinguished because in eternity there are no such differences . . .'[7]

The life of God is thus constituted in a structure of relations, whose contents are narrative. This structure is constrained by a difference between whence and whither, that one cannot finally refrain from calling 'past' and 'future' and that is identical with the distinction between the Father and the Spirit. Thus this difference is not measurable; nothing in God recedes into the past or approaches from the future. Karl Barth says of evil: in the eternal life of God, as he in freedom lives it, evil is ontologically that which is left behind. But the difference is also absolute; there is no perspective from which to see evil as future or the Kingdom as past.[8]

It is standard doctrine that God creates time in that he calls forth creatures. It is perhaps not so regularly noted that if we creatures 'live and move and have our being in God', then time also, in that it is the horizon of our living and moving, cannot be extrinsic to God. Time, I suggest, is the *accommodation* God makes in his living and moving eternity, for others than himself.

II. B.

Aristotle notoriously held that a good story is one in which events occur 'unexpectedly but on account of each other'.[9] If I may unpack and perhaps press his meaning a bit: a good story is one in which each event is in some way or within some range unpredictable before it happens but is greeted with 'But of course' upon its happening. The order of any good story is an ordering by the outcome of the narrated events; within the story there oper-

---

[7] Karl Barth, *Kirchliche Dogmatik* II/1, Die Wirklichkeit Gottes 2. Teil, Zürich: Theologischer Verlag Zürich 1987 (1940), pp. 685–6, 690.
[8] Cf. Robert W. Jenson, *Alpha and Omega: A Study in the Theology of Karl Barth*, New York: Thomas Nelson 1963, pp. 101–11.
[9] Aristotle, *Peri Poietikes* 1452a, 3: *para ten doxan, di' allela*.

ates – here that inevitable cliché again – a power of the future to liberate each successive specious present from mere predictabilities, from being the mere consequence of what has gone before, and to open it to itself, to itself as what is precisely not yet, and is indeed determinately not yet. We may ask: Can this ordering be regarded as a sort of causation? That is, can stories *as* stories be true of reality other than that posited in the story-telling itself? As deconstructionists would put it, does narrative discourse have any body but itself? Or that is again, can Aristotle's criterion of a good story apply to non-fiction?

If we put this question in the general form I just gave it, we ask the great question of Western Christian metaphysics. Nor is the West's metaphysical undertaking much to the side of my assignment. But the immediate question is at once deeper and more specific: Is there such causation in *God* ? Is his life in straightforward fact ordered by an Outcome which is his outcome, and so in a freedom that is more than abstract aseity? The theology of Mediterranean antiquity thought there could be no such causality in God; the gospel must teach us that there is.

There is a specific *locus* in which this teaching must occur. It is because the *Holy Spirit* is distinctly and fully 'one of the Trinity' that God's life is narratively ordered. Indeed, in the specification I just gave of 'narrative causation', I inevitably repeated myself from an earlier passage about the Spirit's triune role. The Spirit is God as the Power of his own and our future; and it is that the Spirit is God as the Power of his own future, as the Power of a future that is truly 'unexpected' and yet connected, also for him, that the Spirit is a distinct identity of and in God.

The Spirit is God as his and our future rushing upon us, he is the eschatological reality of God, the Power as which God is the active Goal of all things, as which God is for himself and for us those 'things hoped for', those 'things not seen', which call for faith and not mere religious assurance. When the creeds' third articles end with the resurrection and the life everlasting, they merely make specific what the Spirit in himself in person is.

It has been the reproach of Orthodoxy against the West,[10] that Western theology does not, in its doctrine of the 'immanent' Trinity, bring the eschatological reality of the Spirit to full expression. I think we must accept the reproach.

---

[10] Cf. Jenson, *Unbaptized God. The Basic Flaw in Ecumenical Theology,* Minneapolis: Fortress Press, pp. 132–7.

To interpret God's reality by the narrative causality that in fact is in him, we must understand and say two things of the Spirit: that he is indeed the Spirit *of* the Father and, thereupon, of the Son; and that he brings otherness and novelty to the Father and the Son. In *himself*, God confronts his own future, he confronts the Spirit who is the Spirit 'of' the Father, as, somehow, 'unexpected', as the novelty of a genuine narrative. There is, I think, something to be said for the Western *'filioque'*, simply as an affirmative proposition – and, of course, apart from the question of its creedal legitimacy. But insofar as the *'filioque'* allows the difference between the Son and the Spirit to be stated geometrically, without necessary reference to the Spirit's place in the biblical narrative, it does indeed express and perpetuate a deeply static interpretation of God.

Orthodoxy's reproach has most frequently been made concrete as a reproach to the West's feeble apprehension of the church: because we – Catholic or Protestant – do not perceive Pentecost as a new step of salvation history, we perceive the church as fundamentally a social reality of this world governed by the same rules and problems as other social realities of the world. Whether we then misconstrue the church in institutionalist or individualist fashion is of secondary importance.

But I would like to suggest another place where the West's feeble celebration of the Spirit has been disastrous. The great occurrence whose causality in God must be of the dramatic sort I have been evoking, is the Resurrection. And that the Resurrection does not *connect* in the story of Salvation as the West tends to tell it, has long been noted and lamented. And nor are this and the previous frailty unconnected.

III.

The point of trinitarian theology is to maintain against all compunctions that the biblical story about God and us is true of and for God himself. I have suggested that trinitarian theology does this in that it says how God has time, and how God's life is like a good play according to Aristotle. There are doubtless other similar points that could as well have been made, but perhaps these will be enough to be going on with.

And I must end as I began – and so in very untrinitarian

fashion: All that can be said about the point that trinitarian theology *has*, will be false unless we simultaneously think the point that trinitarian theology *is*.

2. The Doctrine of the Holy Trinity:
The Significance of the Cappadocian Contribution

John D. Zizioulas

Introduction

Cappadocia, which lies in the heart of Asia Minor, became an important centre of Christian theology in the fourth century AD. Already at the time of St Paul there was a small Christian community in Cappadocia where Christianity spread so rapidly as to produce a number of martyrs and confessors in the second century, and to contribute seven bishops to the Council of Nicaea in AD 325. But it was mainly in the second half of the fourth century that Cappadocia became famous for its theological thought. This was due to four leading figures whose theological and philosophical originality sealed the entire history of Christian thought: St Basil the Great, bishop of Caesarea in Cappadocia (ca. 330–79); St Gregory of Nazianzus, known as the 'Theologian' (ca. 330–89/90), at first briefly bishop of Sassima in Cappadocia and later on, also briefly, Archbishop of Constantinople; St Gregory, the younger brother of Basil, bishop of Nyssa (ca. 335–94?), and, finally, their friend St Amphilochius (340/45 –?), bishop of Iconium. The first three of these left behind them a considerable number of writings (dogmatic treatises, exegetical works, ascetic writings, orations, sermons and letters), which allow us to appreciate their thought, while St Amphilochius' work survives only in a limited number of homilies and letters, some of them only in fragments.

Although the theological contribution of these Cappadocian Fathers is universally recognized and acknowledged, its importance is by no means limited to theology. It involves a radical

44

reorientation of classical Greek humanism, a conception of man and a view of existence, which ancient thought proved unable to produce in spite of its many achievements in philosophy. The occasion for this was offered by the theological controversies of the time, but the implications of the Cappadocian Fathers' contribution reach beyond theology in the strict doctrinal sense and affect the entire culture of late antiquity to such an extent that the whole of Byzantine and European thought would remain incomprehensible without a knowledge of this contribution.

How does the doctrine of God appear, if placed in the light of Cappadocian theology? What problems concerning the doctrine of the Trinity and its philosophical integrity could be overcome with the help of this theology? What consequences does this theology have for our understanding of the human being and of existence as a whole? These kinds of questions are the essential concerns of this paper. Needless to say, however, such vast and complex questions cannot be dealt with in an exhaustive way in such a limited space. Only some suggestions will be put forth and some central ideas underlined. The Cappadocian contribution still awaits its comprehensive and exhaustive treatment in theological – and philosophical – research, in spite of the considerable number of words devoted to its individual representatives.

In order to understand and appreciate correctly the contribution of the Cappadocians to the doctrine of the Trinity we must first set the historical context. What were the Cappadocians reacting against? Why did they take the view they took, and how did they try to respond to the challenges of their contemporaries? After trying to give an answer to these questions we may consider the lasting significance of these Fathers' theology for other times.

I. The Historical Context

If we try to single out the sensitivities – we might call them obsessions – of the Cappadocian Fathers vis-à-vis their contemporaries, we may locate them in the following areas:

A. *Sabellianism*
Sabellianism represented an interpretation of the doctrine of the Trinity which involved the view that the Father, the Son

and the Spirit were not full persons in an ontological sense but *roles* assumed by the one God. Sabellius seems to have used the term person in the singular, implying that there is 'one person' in God.[1] This modalistic interpretation made it impossible to understand how the Son, eternally or in the Incarnation had a relation of reciprocal dialogue with the Father, praying to Him, etc., as the Gospel stories require us to believe. It would also make it impossible for the Christian to establish a fully personal dialogue and relationship with *each* of the three persons of the Trinity. Furthermore, it would appear that God was somehow 'acting' in the Economy, pretending, as it were, to be what He appeared to be, and not revealing or giving to us His true self, His very being.

For these and other reasons the doctrine of the Trinity had to be interpreted in such a way as to exclude any Sabellian or crypto-Sabellian understanding, and the only way to achieve this would be by stressing the fullness and ontological integrity of each person of the Trinity. The Cappadocians were so deeply concerned with this that they went as far as rejecting the use of the term *prosopon* or person to describe the Trinity[2] – a term that had entered theological terminology since Tertullian in the West and found its way into the East probably through Hippolytus – particularly since this term was loaded with connotations of acting on the theatrical stage or playing a role in society, when used in the ancient Graeco-Roman world. In their attempt to protect the doctrine from such connotations the Cappadocians were at times ready to speak of 'three beings' in referring to the Trinity. For the same reason they preferred to use images of the Trinity that would imply the ontological fullness of each person, such as 'three suns', 'three torches', etc. thus introducing a fundamental change in the Nicaean terminology which was inclined towards the use of images indicating one source extended into three ('light of light' etc.). By doing this the Cappadocians came to be known as being interested in the Trinity more than in the unity of God. (Cf. the well-known textbook thesis that the West began with the unity of God and then moved to the Trinity, while the East followed the opposite course.) This stress on the integrity and fullness of the persons

---

[1] Cf. G. L. Prestige, *God in Patristic Thought,* London: SPCK 1936, pp. 113f and 160f.

[2] See Basil, *Ep.* 236, 6.

was full of important philosophical implications, as we shall see later on.

Out of this concern for the ontological integrity of each person in the Trinity came the historic revolution, as I should like to call it,[3] in the history of philosophy, namely the identification of the idea of person with that of *hypostasis*. It would lead us too far to discuss here the history of these terms. Suffice it to recall that only a generation before the Cappadocians the term *hypostasis* was fully identified with that of *ousia* or substance[4] (indeed, the Latin term *substantia* would literally translate into Greek as *hypostasis*). St Athanasius makes it clear that *hypostasis* did not differ from *ousia*, both terms indicating 'being' or 'existence'. The Cappadocians changed this by dissociating *hypostasis* from *ousia* and attaching it to *prosopon*. This was done in order to make the expression 'three persons' free from Sabellian interpretations and thus acceptable to the Cappadocians. That this constitutes an historical revolution in philosophy we shall have an opportunity to point out later, when we discuss the philosophical significance of the Cappadocian contribution.

Now, the Cappadocians seem to have done well with pointing out and defending the fullness and integrity of each person, but what about the unity or oneness of God? Were they not in danger of introducing tritheism?

To avoid this danger the Cappadocians suggested that *ousia* (substance) or *physis* (nature) in God should be taken in the sense of the general category which we apply to more than one person. With the help of Aristotelian philosophy they illustrated this by a reference to the one human nature or substance which is general and is applied to all human beings, and to the many concrete human beings (e.g. John, George, Basil) who are to be called *hypostases* (plural), not natures or substances.[5] In this way they removed all apparent illogicality from their position, since it *is* logically possible to speak of one substance and three *hypostases* (or persons), as the above example shows. But the theological difficulty was there, since in the above example of the one human nature and three (or more) human beings we have to do

---

3 See my *Being as Communion*, London: Darton, Longman & Todd 1985, p. 36f.
4 See Athanasius, *Letter to the Bishops of Egypt and Libya* (PG 26, 1036B).
5 E.g. Basil, *Ep.* 236, 6; 38, 5 etc.

with *three men*, whereas in the Trinity we do not imply three
Gods, but one.

In order to meet this theological difficulty, the Cappadocian
Fathers posed the question of what accounts for the difficulty in
reconciling the one and the three in human existence. This was of
paramount significance anthropologically, as we shall see later.
The reason why human beings cannot be one and many at the
same time involves the following observations.

(a) In human existence nature precedes the person. When John
or George or Basil are born, the one human nature precedes them;
they, therefore, represent and embody only *part* of the human
nature. Through human procreation humanity is *divided,* and no
human person can be said to be the bearer of the totality of human nature. This is why the death of one person does not auto-
matically bring about the death of the rest – or, conversely, the
life of one such person the life of the rest.

(b) Because of this each human person can be conceived as an
individual, i.e. as an entity independent ontologically from
other human beings. The unity between human beings is not ontologically identical with their diversity or multiplicity.The one
and the many do not coincide. It is this existential difficulty
that leads to the logical difficulty of saying 'one' and 'many'
with the same breath.

Now, if we contrast this with God's existence, we see immediately that this existential and hence logical difficulty is
not applicable to God. Since God by definition has not had a
beginning, and space and time do not enter His existence, the
three persons of the Trinity do not share a pre-existing or
logically prior to them divine nature, but coincide with it.
Multiplicity in God does not involve a division of His nature, as
happens with man.[6]

It is impossible, therefore, to say that in God, as it is the case
with human beings, nature precedes the person. Equally and for
the same reasons it is impossible to say that in God any of the
three persons exist or can exist in separation from the other persons. The three constitute such an unbreakable unity that individualism is absolutely inconceivable in their case. The three
persons of the Trinity are thus one God, because they are so
united in an unbreakable communion (*koinonia*) that none of

---

[6] E.g. Gregory of Nyssa, *Quod non sint tres . . .* (PG 45, 125).

them can be conceived apart from the rest. The mystery of the one God in three persons points to a way of being which precludes individualism and separation (or self-sufficiency and self-existence) as a criterion of multiplicity. The 'one' not only does not precede – logically or otherwise – the 'many', but, on the contrary, requires the 'many' from the very start in order to exist.

This, therefore, seems to be the great innovation in philosophical thought, brought about by the Cappadocian Trinitarian theology, which carries with it a decisively new way of conceiving human existence, as we shall see later.

B. *Eunomianism*

Eunomianism marked a problematic unknown to Athanasius and Nicaea, since it introduced a far more sophisticated philosophical argument than original Arianism had done. Eunomius, who came himself from Cappadocia, was made by the Arians Bishop of Cyzicus, and was the most radical and perhaps the most sophisticated of the extreme Arians known as Anomoeans. In order to prove by way of Aristotelian dialectic that the Son is totally *unlike* the Father, the Eunomians placed the substance of God in being unbegotten (*agennetos*) and concluded that since the Son is 'begotten' (Nicaea itself called him so) he falls outside the being or substance of God.

The refutation of such an argument requires that we make a sharp distinction between substance and person in God. By being a person the Father was to be distinguished from divine substance, and thus it would be wrong to conclude that the Son is not God or *homoousios* with the Father. When God is called Father or 'unbegotten' He is called so not with reference to His substance, but to personhood. Indeed, about the substance of God nothing can be said at all: no property or quality is applicable, except that it is one, undivided and absolutely simple and uncompounded, descriptions pointing to total unknowability rather than knowledge of the divine substance. If there are any properties (*idiomata*) that can be spoken of in God these are applicable to His personhood, such as unbegottenness or Fatherhood for the Father, begottenness or Sonship of the Son and *ekporeusis* (spiration) of the Spirit. These personal or hypostatic properties are incommunicable – unbegottenness being precisely one of them – whereas substance is communicated among the three persons. A person is thus defined through properties which are absolutely *unique*, and in this respect differs fundamentally from nature or substance. The reaction against Eunomianism produced, therefore, on the one hand a clear and fundamental distinction between person and nature, thus allowing the concept of person to emerge more clearly as a distinct category in ontology, and on the other hand underlined the idea that personhood can be known and identified through its absolute uniqueness and irreplaceability, something that has not ceased to be of existential relevance in philosophy.

Now, this incommunicability of hypostatic properties does not mean that persons in the Trinity are to be understood as autonomous individuals. We must beware of making this incommunicability the definition of person *par excellence*, as Richard of St. Victor seems to do, for although the hypostatic properties are not communicated, the notion of the person is inconceivable outside a relationship. The Cappadocians called the persons by names indicating *schesis* (relationship)[7]: none of the three persons can be conceived without reference to the other two, both logically and ontologically. The problem is how to reconcile incommunicability with relationship, but this again is a matter of freeing divine existence from the servitude of personhood to substance, a servitude which applies only to created existence. By being uncreated, the three persons are not faced with a given substance, but exist freely. Being is simultaneously relational and hypostatic. But this leads us to a consideration of the philosophical consequences of Cappadocian theology.

II. The Philosophical Implications

Here again history must give us the starting point. It is normally assumed that the Greek Fathers were Platonic or Aristotelian in their thinking, and yet a careful study of them would reveal that they were as obsessed with Greek philosophy as they were with various heretical ideas of their time. The doctrine of the Trinity offered the occasion to the Cappadocians to express their distance both explicitly and implicitly from Platonism in particular and thus introduce a new philosophy.

---

[7] E.g. Gregory Naz., *Or.* 29 (PG 36, 96): 'The Father is a name neither of substance nor of energy but of *schesis*'.

One of the references to Plato made by St Gregory of Nazianzus is worthy of particular mention. He refers at one point to the philosopher as having spoken of God as a crater which overflows with goodness and love, and rejects this image as implying a process of natural or substantial and therefore necessary, generation of existence. Gregory would not like to see the generation of the Son or the spiration of the Spirit understood in such terms, i.e. by way of a substantial growth. (Here we may perhaps observe some departure from the Athanasian idea of the 'fertile substance of God'.) He would insist, together with the rest of the Cappadocians, that the *cause* or *aition* of divine existence is the Father, which means a person, for this would make the Trinity a matter of ontological freedom. In fact in one of his theological orations Gregory takes up the defence of Nicaea against the Arian accusation that the *homoousios* implies necessity in God's being and develops it further than Athanasius – who in fact said very little on this matter – by stressing the role of the *Father* as the cause of divine being. Generation (and spiration) are not necessary but free because although there is one will 'concurrent' (as St Cyril of Alexandria would say)[8] with the divine substance, there is the 'willing one' (*ho thelon*)[9] and that is the Father. By making the Father the only cause of divine existence the Cappadocians aimed at understanding freedom in ontology, something that Greek philosophy had never done before.

It is in the light of this observation that we can appreciate two more points emerging from the study of the sources. The first is a 'detail' that we observe in the Creed of Nicaea-Constantinople, a detail dismissed normally by historians of doctrine (e.g. Kelly)[10] as insignificant. I am referring to the fact that the Council of Constantinople of AD 381, operating clearly under Cappadocian influence – Gregory of Nazianzus, then Archbishop of Constantinople, was presiding over it for a time – took the bold step of altering the Creed of Nicaea at the point where it referred to the Son as being 'from the substance of the Father' (*ek tes ousias tou patros*) and making it simply read 'from the Father' (*ek tou patros*). This change at a time when

---

8 Cyril Alex., *De Trin.* 2.
9 Thus Gregory Naz., *Or. theol.* 3, 5–7.
10 Cf. J. N. D. Kelly, *Early Christian Creeds*, London: Longmans 1950, p. 333.

fights took place over words could not be accidental. It is a clear
expression of the Cappadocian interest in stressing that it is the
person of the Father and not divine substance that is the source
and cause of the Trinity.

The other point relates to the content that the term
monarchia finally received in the Greek Fathers. The one *arche*
in God came to be understood ontologically, i.e. in terms of
origination of being, and was attached to the person of the
Father. The 'one God' is the Father[11], and not the one substance,
as Augustine and medieval Scholasticism would say. This puts
the person of the Father in the place of the one God, and suggests
a kind of monotheism which is not only Biblical but also more
akin to Trinitarian theology. If, therefore, we wish to follow
the Cappadocians in their understanding of the Trinity in
relation to monotheism, we must adopt an ontology which is
based on personhood, i.e. on a unity or openness emerging from
relationships, and not one of substance, i.e. of the self-existent
and in the final analysis individualistic being. The philosophical scandal of the Trinity can be resolved or accepted only if
substance gives way to personhood as the causing principle or
arche in ontology.

I have called the Cappadocians revolutionary thinkers in
the history of philosophy. This would emerge from a hasty
survey of ancient Greek thought in relation to that of the
Cappadocians.

Ancient Greek thought in all its variations, ever since the
pre-Socratic philosophers and up to and including Neoplatonism, tended to give priority to the 'one' over the 'many'. At
the time of the Greek Fathers this had taken several forms,
some of them more theological and some more philosophical. On
the theological level the predominant pagan Greek philosophy
at the time of the Cappadocian Fathers, namely Neoplatonism,
had identified the 'One' with God Himself, considering the
multiplicity of beings, the 'many', to be emanations basically of
a degrading nature, so that the return to the 'One' through the
recollection of the soul was thought to be the purpose and aim of

---

[11] See e.g. Gregory Naz., *Or.* 42, 15. Cf. G. L. Prestige, op. cit., p. 254: '. . .
their (the three Persons') ground of unity (*henwsis*) is the Father, out of
whom and towards whom are reckoned the subsequent Persons, not as to
confuse them but so as to attach them. The doctrine of monarchy had begun
by basing the unity of God on the single Person of the Father . . .'

all existence. Earlier on in the first century Philo, whose significance as the link between classical Platonism and Neoplatonism
was decisive, had argued that God is the only true 'One' because
He is the only one who is truly 'alone'. The doctrine of the Holy
Trinity as developed by the Cappadocians ran counter to this
priority and exaltation of the 'One' over the 'Many' in philosophy.

With regard to human existence, too, classical Greek philosophy at that time had given priority to nature over particular
persons. The views current at the time of the Cappadocian Fathers were either of a Platonic or of an Aristotelian kind. The
first spoke of human nature as an ideal humanity, a *genos
hyperkeimenon*, whose image every human being is, whereas
the latter preferred to give priority to a substratum of the human species, *a genos hypokeimenon*, from which the various
human beings emerge.[12] In both cases man in his diversity and
plurality of persons was subject to the necessity – or priority – of
his nature. Nature or substance always preceded the person in
classical Greek thought.

The Cappadocian Fathers challenged this established view
of philosophy through their Trinitarian theology. They
claimed that the priority of nature over the person, or of the
'one' over the 'many', is due to the fact that human existence is
a *created* existence, i.e. it is an existence with a beginning , and
should not be made into a metaphysical principle. True being in
its genuine metaphysical state, which concerns philosophy *par
excellence*, is to be found in God, whose uncreated existence does
not involve the priority of the 'One' or of nature over the 'Many'
or the persons. The way in which God exists involves simultaneously the 'One' and the 'Many', and this means that the
person has to be given ontological primacy in philosophy.

To give ontological primacy to the person would mean to undo
the fundamental principles with which Greek philosophy had
operated since its inception.The particular person never had an
ontological role in classical Greek thought. What mattered ultimately was the unity or totality of being of which man was but
a portion. Plato in addressing the particular being makes it clear

---

12 See Basil, *Ep.* 361 and 362. For a discussion of these letters and their
philosophical significance see my 'On Being a Person: Towards an
Ontology of Personhood' in Chr. Schwöbel and C. E. Gunton (eds.),
Persons: Human and Divine, Edinburgh: T&T Clark 1991, pp. 37ff.

that 'the whole was not brought into being for thy sake, but thou art brought for its sake'. With a striking consistency classical Greek tragedy invited man – and even the gods – to succumb to the order and justice that held the universe together, so that *kosmos* (meaning both natural order and proper behaviour) may prevail. Underneath the variety of beings, the 'many', there is the one Reason (*Logos*) that gives them their significance in existence. No digression from this one Reason can be allowed for the 'many' or for the particular beings without a disruption of being, even the very being of these particular beings.

The Trinitarian theology of the Cappadocian Fathers involved a philosophy in which the particular was not secondary to being or nature; it was thus *free* in an absolute sense. In classical thought freedom was cherished as a quality of the individual but not in an ontological sense. The person was free to express his views but was obliged to succumb finally to the common Reason, the *xunos logos* of Heraclitus. Furthermore, the possibility that the person might pose the question of his freedom from *his very existence* was entirely inconceivable in ancient philosophy. It was in fact first raised in modern times by Dostoevsky and other modern existentialist philosophers. Freedom in antiquity always had a restricted moral sense, and did not involve the question of the *being* of the world, which was a 'given' and an external reality for the Greeks. On the contrary, for the Fathers the world's being was due to the freedom of a person, God. *Freedom* is the 'cause' of being for Patristic thought.[13]

Cappadocian theology stressed this principle of freedom as a presupposition of being by extending it to cover the being of God Himself. This was a great innovation of the Cappadocian Fathers, even with regard to their Christian predecessors. The Cappadocian Fathers for the first time in history introduced into the being of God the concept of cause (*aition*), in order to attach it significantly not to the 'one' (God's nature) – but to a *person*, the Father. By distinguishing carefully and persistently between the nature of God and God as the Father they thought that *what causes God to be is the Person of the Father*, not the one divine substance. By so doing they gave to the person onto-

---

[13] For further discussion see my *Being as Communion*, London: Darton, Longman & Todd 1985, esp. ch. 1.

logical priority, and thus freed existence from the logical necessity of substance, of the 'self-existent'. This was a revolutionary step in philosophy, the anthropological consequences of which must not pass unnoticed.

III. The Anthropological Consequences

Man, for the Fathers, is the 'image of God'. He is not God by nature, since he is *created*, i.e. he has had a beginning, and thus is subject to the limitations of space and time which involve individuation and ultimately death. Nevertheless, he is called to exist in the way God exists.

In order to understand this we must consider the distinction made by the Cappadocian Fathers between nature and person or 'mode of existence' (*tropos hyparxeos*), as they called it. Nature or substance points to the simple fact that something exists, to the *what* (*ti*) of something. It can be predicated of more than one thing. Person or *hypostasis*, on the other hand, points to *how* (*hopos* or *pos*) and can only be predicated of one being, and this in an absolute sense. When we consider human nature (or substance: *ousia*), we refer it to all human beings; there is nothing unique about having a human nature. Furthermore, all the 'natural' characteristics of human nature such as dividedness – and hence individuation leading to decomposition and finally death – are all aspects of human 'substance' and determine the human being as far as its nature is concerned. It is the *how* of human nature, i.e. personhood, that by acquiring the role of ontological cause, as is the case with God's being, determines whether nature's limitations will finally be overcome or not. The 'image of God' in man has precisely to do with this *how*, not with the *what* man is; it relates not to nature – man can never become God by nature – but to personhood. This means that man is free to affect the *how* of his existence either in the direction of the way (the *how*) God is, or in the direction of *what* his, i.e. man's nature is. Living according to nature (*kata physin*) would thus amount to individualism, mortality, etc., since man is not immortal *kata physin*. Living, on the other hand, according to the image of God means living in the way God exists, i.e. as an image of God's personhood, and this would amount to 'becoming God'. This is what the *theosis* of man means in the thinking of the Greek Fathers.

It follows from this that although man's nature is ontologically prior to his personhood, as we have already noted, man is called to an effort to free himself from the necessity of his nature and behave in all respects as if the person were free from the laws of nature. In practical terms this is what the Fathers saw in the *ascetic* effort which they regarded as essential to all human existence, regardless of whether one was a monk or lived in the world. Without an attempt to free the person from the necessity of nature one cannot be the 'image of God', since in God, as we have noted above, the person, and not nature, causes Him to be way He is.

The essence, therefore, of the anthropology which results from the Trinitarian theology of the Cappadocian Fathers lies in the significance of personhood in human existence. The Cappadocian Fathers gave to the world the most precious concept it possesses: *the concept of the person, as an ontological concept in the ultimate sense.* Since this concept has become, at least in principle, not only part of our Christian heritage but also an ideal of our culture in general, it may be useful to remind ourselves of its exact content and significance as it emerges from a study of the theology of the Cappadocians.

(a) As it emerges from the way personhood is understood by the Cappadocian Fathers with reference to God, the person is not a secondary but a primary and absolute notion in existence. Nothing is more sacred than the person since it constitutes the 'way of being' of God Himself. The person cannot be sacrificed or subjected to any ideal, to any moral or natural order, or to any expediency or objective, even of the most sacred kind. In order to *be truly* and *be yourself,* you must be a person, i.e. you must be free from and higher than any necessity or objective – natural, moral, religious or ideological. What gives meaning and value to existence is the person as absolute freedom.

(b) The person cannot exist in isolation. God is not alone; He is *communion.* Love is not a feeling, a sentiment springing from nature like a flower from a tree. Love is a *relationship,* it is the free coming out of one's self, the breaking of one's will, a *free* submission to the will of another. It is the other and our relationship with him that gives us our identity, our otherness, making us 'who we are', i.e. persons; for by being an inseparable part of a relationship that matters ontologically we emerge as *unique* and *irreplaceable* entities. This, therefore, is what accounts for our being, and our being ourselves and not someone else: our personhood. It is in this that the 'reason', the *logos* of our being lies: in the relationship of love that makes us unique and irreplaceable *for another*. The *logos* that accounts for God's being is the uniquely beloved Son, and it is through this loving relationship that God, too, or rather God *par excellence*, e-merges as unique and irreplaceable by being eternally the Fa-ther of a unique (*monogenes*) Son. This is the great message of the Patristic idea of the person. The *raison d'être* , the *logos tou einai* of each one's being, for which the Greek mind was always searching, is not to be found in the *nature* of this being, but in the *person*, i.e. in the identity created freely by love and not by the necessity of its self-existence. As a person you exist as long as you love and you are loved. When you are treated as nature, as a thing, you die as a particular identity. And if your soul is im-mortal, what is the use? You will exist, but without a personal identity; you will be eternally dying in the hell of anonymity, in the Hades of immortal souls. For nature in itself cannot give you existence and being as an absolutely unique and particular identity. Nature always points to the general; it is the person that safeguards uniqueness and absolute particularity. The im-mortality, therefore, of one's soul, even if it implies existence, cannot imply personal identity in the true sense. Now that we know, thanks to the Patristic theology of personhood, how God exists, we know what it means truly to exist as a particular being. As images of God we are persons, not natures: there can never be an image of the *nature* of God, nor would it be a welcome thing for humanity to be absorbed in divine nature. Only when in this life we exist as persons can we hope to live eternally in the true, personal sense. This means that exactly as is the case with God, so with us, too: personal identity can emerge only from love as freedom and from freedom as love.

(c) The person is something *unique* and *unrepeatable*. Nature and species are perpetuated and replaceable. Individuals taken as nature or species are never absolutely unique. They can be similar; they can be composed and decomposed; they can be com-bined with others in order to produce results or even new species; they can be used to serve purposes – sacred or not, this does not matter. On the contrary, persons can neither be reproduced nor perpetuated like species; they cannot be composed or decom-posed, combined or used for any objective whatsoever – even the

most sacred one. Whosoever treats a person in such ways auto-
matically turns him into a thing, he dissolves and brings into
non-existence his *personal particularity*. If one does not see one's
fellow human being as the image of God *in this sense*, i.e. as a
person, then one cannot see this being as a truly eternal identity.
For death dissolves us all into one indistinguishable nature,
turning us into 'substance', or things. What gives us an identity
that does not die is not our nature but our personal relationship
with God's undying personal identity. Only when nature is
hypostatic or personal, as is the case with God, does it exist
truly and eternally. For it is only then that it acquires uniqueness and becomes an unrepeatable and irreplaceable particularity in the 'mode of being' which we find in the Trinity.

Conclusion

If we are allowed or even incited in our culture to think or hope
for true personhood in human existence, we owe it above all to
the Christian thought that Cappadocia produced in the fourth
century. The Cappadocian Church Fathers developed and bequeathed to us a concept of God, who exists as a communion of
free love out of which unique, irreplaceable and unrepeatable
identities emerge, i.e. true persons in the absolute ontological
sense. It is of such a God that man is meant to be an 'image'.
There is no higher and fuller anthropology than this anthropology of true and full personhood.
    Modern man tends on the whole to think highly of an anthro-
pology of personhood, but the common and widespread assumptions as to what a person is are by no means consonant with what
we have seen emerging from a study of the Cappadocian Fathers. Most of us today, when we say 'person' mean an *individual*. This goes back to St Augustine, and especially to Boethius in
the fifth century AD, who defined the person as an individual
nature endowed with rationality and consciousness. Throughout
the entire history of Western thought the equation of person
with the thinking, self-conscious individual has led to a culture
in which the thinking individual has become the highest
concept in anthropology. This is not what emerges from the
thought of the Cappadocian Fathers. It is rather the opposite of
this that results from a study of their thought. For according to
it, true personhood arises not from one's individualistic isolation

from others but from love and relationship with others, from communion. Love alone, free love, unqualified by natural necessities, can generate personhood. This is true of God whose being, as the Cappadocian Fathers saw it, is constituted and 'hypostasized' through a free event of love caused by a free and loving person, the Father, and not by the necessity of divine nature. This is true also of man who is called to exercise his freedom as love and his love as freedom, and thus show himself to be the 'image of God'.

In our times several attempts are being made by Western philosophers to correct the Western equation of the 'person' with the 'individual'.[14] Christianity's encounter with other religions, such as Buddhism, is forcing people to reconsider this traditional individualistic view of personhood. Today, then, is perhaps the most appropriate time to go back to a deeper study and appreciation of the fruits of Christian thought produced in Cappadocia in the fourth century, the most important of which is undoubtedly the idea of the person, as the Cappadocian Fathers saw and developed it.

This, therefore, is the existential – in the broader sense – significance of the Cappadocian contribution to Trinitarian theology: it makes us see in God a kind of existence we all want to lead; it is therefore basically a soteriological theology. But I think the Cappadocians have also something to say to some of today's issues concerning the doctrine of God. I refer particularly to the issues raised by feminist theology, especially concerning the use of names for God. The Cappadocians, in accordance with the apophatic tradition of the East, would say that all language concerning the substance of God and its qualities or energies is bound to be inadequate. Yet a distinction must be made between nature and person also at the level of human discourse. The names Father, Son and Spirit are indicative of *personal* identity. And since these are the *only* names that indicate personal identity they cannot be changed. Names indicating energies are changeable (e.g. God is good, or powerful, for example), because they are all drawn from our experience, which cannot adequately describe God. But what about Father, Son and Spirit – are they drawn from experience? Is there any analogy

---

14 Thus, J. Macmurray, *The Self as Agent*, London: Faber & Faber 1957, and *Persons in Relation*, London: Faber & Faber 1961.

possible between God's Fatherhood and human fatherhood? There may be something of an analogy in what concerns moral qualities attached to Fatherhood (Creator, loving and caring person, etc.). But these are not *personal* properties – they apply to all three persons of the Trinity, i.e. to the common substance or energy. Father, Son and Spirit are names of personal identity, names by which God in Christ reveals Himself and names Himself for us. This is the big difference between Trinitarian language and even the appellation 'God', which, in the sense of *divinitas*, is not a name of God. Only as Person is He nameable. But His name is known and revealed to us only in Christ, which means only in and through the Father-Son relationship. He is therefore only known as Father.

The distinction between nature and person is, therefore, crucial also with regard to the issue of what is called 'comprehensive language'. Equally, it is crucial whether we identify the one God with the Father or with the one substance. For if He is Father only secondarily and not in His ultimate personal identity, Fatherhood is not the name *of* God but a name *about* God. In this case it can be changed so as to convey better the message we wish to convey about God's being.

The Cappadocians have taught us that the Trinity is not a matter for academic speculation, but for personal relationship. As such, it is truth revealed only by participation in the Father-Son relationship through the Spirit which allows us to cry '*Abba*, Father'. The Trinity is therefore revealed only in the church, i.e. the community through which we become sons of the Father of Jesus Christ. Outside this it remains a stumbling block and a scandal.

3. Trinity, Logic and Ontology

John Heywood Thomas

My original purpose in choosing this topic was to say something about two issues simply – the logicality of the assertion of the dogma that God is triune and the coherence of a metaphysic which talks of personal relations within a substantial unity. Quite clearly neither of these issues is simple and that task is one of sufficient difficulty. However, as in all matters of doctrine it is really impossible to treat our problems as though they were capable of being abstracted from the context of history and being considered as purely speculative issues. It might seem that what I am saying here is the kind of thing that R. G. Collingwood long ago argued, that there is a tendency in discussion of philosophical problems to treat as irrelevant the issue whether what is being debated had ever been asserted. Collingwood speaks in *An Autobiography* of the Oxford philosophy of his day needing a background of sound scholarship. 'I therefore taught my pupils, more by example than by precept, that they must never accept any criticism of anybody's philosophy which they might hear or read without satisfying themselves by firsthand study that this was the philosophy he actually expounded.'[1] Collingwood goes on to show how such an activity is more than the simple consultation of a text. Those eminent philosophers Rosenkrantz and Guildernstern seem to think that a text such as *Parmenides* is easier to understand than 'a rotten little Roman fort'.[2] He goes on to elaborate this view of philosophy as 'Question and answer' and to enunciate his principle of the history of philosophy.

> By degrees I found that there was no recognised branch of philosophy to which the principle did not apply that its problems, as well as the solutions proposed for them, had their own history. The conception of 'eternal problems' disappeared entirely, except so far

---

[1] R. G. Collingwood, *An Autobiography*, Harmondsworth: Penguin Books 1944, p. 23.
[2] Ibid., p. 31.

as any historical fact could be called eternal because it had happened once for all.

Having thus with regard to the supposed permanence of philosophical problems found the 'realist' conception of philosophical history false at every point where I could think of testing it, I turned to another aspect of the same conception: namely the 'realists' distinction between the 'historical' question 'what was so-and-so's theory on such and such a matter?' and the 'philosophical' question 'was he right?'

This distinction was soon condemned as fallacious . . .[We] cannot fish the problem P out of the hyperuranian lucky-bag, hold it up, and say 'What did so-and-so think about this?' We have to begin, as poor devils of historians begin, from the other end . . .We have to say 'here is a passage of Leibniz what is the problem with which it deals?' Perhaps we label that problem P14. Then comes the question 'Does Leibniz deal with P14 rightly or wrongly?' The answer to this is not quite so simple as the 'realists' think.[3]

I have always been convinced that the progress of theology throughout the ages has been much more human and indeed social than the kind of thing which made History of Doctrine seem to me as an undergraduate the strangest combination of sophistry and gobble-de-gook. Consequently I think that there is much in these remarks of Collingwood's that is instructive for the writing of a history of doctrine. In so far as I shall be driven to some historical comment I hope to have read, marked and inwardly digested. Yet the most important sense in which we are here involved in the concretions of history is that the issue of the Trinity would not arise for us were it not that the faith we discuss is directed towards the God revealed in history. In other words, Trinity is our belief in our 'creation, preservation and redemption' as these are made clear in the face of Christ. I am very conscious of the fact that I am not making my point plain; but it is at least partly because faith is so much more complicated than the simple issue that Schleiermacher raised – whether a religion is historical or not. Newman saw this very well and that is why he put on the title page of *Grammar of Assent* the remark of St Ambrose – '*Non in dialectica complacuit Deum salvere mundum*'. The point I am feeling for, then, is that when we talk of the relation of Trinitarian doctrine to logic we shall need to look carefully at the kind of logic we are treating. What I can see clearly – no matter how confused is my understanding of all that can be said about the way in which logic has played a part in Trinitarian doctrine – is that very different

[3] Ibid., p. 50.

logics are involved when we ask (i) for a definition of the relation of God the Father to the Son and the Spirit in themselves and (ii) for a clarification of the relation of God in Himself to His creative and salvific work and (iii) the logical form of the inference from the history of salvation to the belief in Trinity and again (iv) the logic of our belief in the Triune God our Creator and Redeemer.

This point needs some explanation despite the fact that a proper account of the matter could launch the discussion in an entirely different direction. The point is that we are in the first place using the term 'logic' both in its strict sense and also in its enlarged sense when we make such a comment as this. Secondly, even when we are treating only issues of formal logic these are different in kind. Thus the first point is clear from the contrast between the final issue listed, and the preceding ones' largely ontological analysis arise from the more formal considerations of (i) and (ii). Yet it should be noted that in (i) the quest is of a definition or a relation that is implicit in our use of the term 'God ' *simpliciter* whereas in (ii) we are looking at that concept used in conjunction with other language that will necessarily involve some kind of factual claim. Finally, the third problem illustrates the way in which, though the foundations of doctrine are never far removed from history, the nature of doctrine cannot be regarded as some kind of empirical generalization so that the normal definition of the inference is a fundamental problem of theological method as such.

Convinced as I am of what might be called the concreteness and humanity of theology I am also sure that the part played by logic in its development as a subject and not merely in the development of doctrine has been crucial. Thus it seems to me that the very emergence of theology as an academic discipline is due to the flowering of logic in the eleventh and twelfth centuries. In these enlightened times we are prone to mock the old tendency to regard medieval philosophy as a barren period riddled with the question of universals as its only concern. Surprisingly perhaps the mistake had much to commend it;for the problem not only did indeed figure very prominently in any and every philosophical discussion during the Middle Ages but did so for a very interesting philosophical reason. This is that the central metaphysical problem bequeathed the Middle Ages by Aristotle's logic or categories was the problem of essence. It is precisely the special way in which such logical problems and their discussion were vested with theological significance that marks the innovative discussions of theology as it developed from the twelfth century onwards.For it was at that point that the study which had already thus been heavily influenced by logic became an academic discipline, 'theologia' not being a term commonly used before that date to refer to it . As G. R. Evans remarks in *Old Arts and New Theology*, remarkable though it may seem that a comparatively few thinkers were responsible, their achievement was 'to bring to light the principles which were to direct the academic study of theology and the arts for several generations'.[4] In the 'Conclusion' she further remarks that the 'overall order and structure' of the *Summa Sententiarum* is already 'marked by the concern for logical or hierarchical unfolding of one topic out of another which Aquinas perfected in the *Summa Theologiae*'.[5]

Even so, what is more significant for our purpose is the contribution of logic to the development of Trinitarian doctrine. It will be hardly be a surprise for anyone in the light of what I have said already that I see this contribution to be of various kinds. Doctrine has, I think, been born of logic as Christianity turned the whole world of philosophy upside down. I think of the old logical formula *ex nihilo nihil* which is clearly the source of the great formulation of faith in Creation as the dogma *creatio ex nihilo*.[6] It is well known that Stoic logic proved invaluable for apologists such as Tertullian in the elaboration and defence of an orthodox Christology.[7] Then Boethius' *Contra Eutychen et Nestorium* is an example of what might be called logic resolving controversy.[8] It is not my aim – even if I were able to claim the competence – to offer an account of the historical interrelations of logic to Trinitarian theology; but there are interesting features which can be noted by someone like myself who has the ability to understand the obvious. The legacy of Boethius was a logical apparatus which facilitated the extraordinary momentum of

---

[4] G. R. Evans, *Old Arts and New Theology. The Beginnings of Theology as an Academic Discipline*, Oxford: Clarendon Press 1980 , p. 14.
[5] Ibid., p. 22f.
[6] Justin Martyr, *Second Dialogue With Trypho*.
[7] Tertullian, *De Carne Christi* and *Adversus Praxean*.
[8] H. M. Barrett, *Boethius, Some Aspects of his Times and Work*, New York 1965, p. 143; and H. Chadwick, *Boethius: the Consolations of Music, Logic, Theology and Philosophy*, Oxford: Clarendon Press 1981, pp. 180–90.

Anselm's thought as that fed as much on his reading of the secular arts as on his reading of Fathers such as Augustine.[9] Anselm is a particularly interesting case because he raised the problem of Trinity with reference to the logical issue of relations and the impossibility of contradictory predication;but this was not the only thing done in the work concerned with Incarnation (*De Incarnatione Verbi*), and it must also be remembered that his exposition of the main points of the doctrine of the Trinity is undertaken as he embarks on his elaboration of what is involved in the procession of the Spirit (*De Processione Spiritus Sancti*).

G. R. Evans has pointed out how limited – perhaps deliberately so – Anselm's theology is in its scope and how this in fact contributes to his remarkable consistency.[10] His policy was to go back to first principles, beginning with essentials and working out the implication of a few doctrinal statements thoroughly. Of that superb logical thoroughness nothing is a better example than the way in which the surprisingly long section of *Monologion* dealing with the Trinity forms the basis of what he says to a very different purpose in *De Incarnatione Verbi*. Since our concern now is not to give an account of these thinkers but simply to call attention to the relevance of logic, it is sufficient to note that what Anselm has called attention to is some logical points of great significance. They are, I think, threefold: first, that properties are different from relations; secondly, that doctrine is elaborated by a certain frame of mind – the logic of the words 'God the Trinity' is that we cannot talk of God except in the language of worship; thirdly, the interrelation of the positive rationality of orthodoxy with the folly of irrational inconsistency springing from heresy or – to put the matter simply – since the orthodox doctrine is rational then the logical inference which demonstrates this is the falsity of its negation.

My last example is St Thomas Aquinas since his thought represents the fullest use of Aristotelian logic and metaphysics in the Middle Ages. He remoulded and rethought materials which were already to hand so that very often his originality consists

9 D. P. Henry, *A Commentary on the De Grammatico of St Anselm*, Dordrecht: Reidel 1974.
10 G. R. Evans, *Anselm and Talking about God*, Oxford: Clarendon Press 1978, pp. 11–12.

not in the novelty of what is said but in the perception and elaboration of conclusions. This is why his work was so often and so
wrongly spoken of as a synthesis of theology and Aristotelianism
when in fact as a devout and orthodox believer he was anxious to
preserve the integrity of revealed theology. Thomas' treatment
of the Trinity is to be found mainly in the *Commentary on the
Sentences*, the *Summa Contra Gentiles* and the *Summa Theologiae*. It is to the last I shall refer. From what I have said
already it is obvious that I want to emphasize Thomas' starting-
point in revelation. Indeed he himself insists that the belief in
the Trinity is neither a matter of demonstration nor of probable
knowledge.[11] As he says in *Summa Theologiae*,[12] by natural
reason 'we can know what belongs to the unity of essence but not
what belongs to the distinctions of the persons'. Therefore 'the
philosophers did not know the mystery of the Trinity of the divine persons by its proper attributes, namely paternity, filiation
and procession' though 'they knew some of the essential attributes appropriate to the persons as power to the Father, wisdom to the Son, and goodness to the Holy Spirit'.[13] He adds
what seems a criticism of the Augustinian analogy of the mind,
saying,[14] 'Nor is the divine image in the intellect an adequate
proof about anything in God since intellect is not in God and ourselves univocally'.

Thomas' intention in his theology, as he tells us, was to revise
or correct Augustine's as Aristotelianism showed this to be nec-
essary.So in regard to Trinity he seeks the aid of both logic and
ontology to set out what is essentially Augustine's theology in a
logical order. Making distinctions between concepts he then
produces what might be called a map of the doctrine. There are
in God, he says, two and only two processions,[15] four and only four
real relations,[16] three and only three persons,[17] five notions[18]
and visible and invisible missions of the Holy Spirit.[19] There is

---

[11] *In Boeth de Trin.* 1.4.
[12] Thomas Aquinas, *Summa Theologiae*, I, 32.1.
[13] Ibid., ad 1.
[14] Ibid., ad 2.
[15] *Summa Theologiae*, I, 27.
[16] Ibid., I, 28.
[17] Ibid., I, 29, 30.
[18] Ibid., I, 32.
[19] Ibid., I, 43.

a tension between the Boethian doctrine of the person and the doctrine enunciated in *De Trinitate* 33 i, ii that the Father is the principium of Godhead, as Hodgson pointed out long ago.[20] But the most significant point is that Thomas' aim is to show the reality of the relations he distinguished.

A further example of Thomas' philosophically sophisticated use of logic is his differentiation between divine generation and divine procession. Generation, he says, properly understood 'signifies the origin of a living being from a confused living principle ... by way of likeness in the same specific nature'.[21]But the word proceeds by way of intelligible action which is a vital operation – from a conjoined principle by way of likeness – because the conception of the intellect is a likeness of the object conceived, and it exists in the same nature because in God understanding and being are the same. Hence the procession of the Word in God is called generation and the preceding Word is called the Son.[22] But the second procession, 'the procession of love in God ought not to be called generation' for 'the procession of the intellect is by way of likeness and so can be called generation because every generation generates its own like whereas the procession of the will is not by way of likeness but is rather by way of impulse and movement towards something. So what proceeds in God by way of love does not proceed as begotten or as a Son but rather as Spirit'.[23] There are, then, for Thomas four real relations in God – paternity, filiation, spiration, procession – identified with the divine essence in their *esse*; but only three of them (paternity, filiation and procession) are really distinct from one another by reason of their mutual opposition.[24] These are the three persons. What is noteworthy about *Summa Theologiae*, then, is the way in which there is a clear perception of the difference between substance and relation. There being three relations in God that are really distinct from one another these are nevertheless really identified with the one simple divine essence. As Thomas puts it pithily – 'as in God there is a real relation there must also be a real opposition. But the very nature of relative

[20] Leonard Hodgson, *The Doctrine of the Trinity*, London: Nisbet 1943, p. 159.
[21] *Summa Theologiae* , I, 27, 2.
[22] Ibid.
[23] Ibid., 4.
[24] Ibid., 28, 1–4.

opposition includes distinction. Hence there must be real distinction in God not according to what is absolute – namely essence, in which there is supreme unity and simplicity, but according to what is relative'.[25] One final point may be made about this use of logic and ontology by Thomas and that is the quite simple assertion that he remained faithful to what seems to me the essentially agnostic stance of his philosophical theology. When he speaks of the need for this knowledge of the divine nature in Question 32 the first reason he advances is that we should have the right idea of creation and the second is itself the intellectual scandal of salvation.

What I have tried to do is to show that in the development of Trinitarian doctrine logic has of necessity been used to elaborate the point of the doctrine as one showing God essentially in relation. In the brief indication of how that was done I also showed that this necessitated recourse to the language of ontology. I now turn to a more systematic discussion. Clearly the main question for logic in regard to the Trinity is that of relation. If the assertion is not the contradictory one that 1=3 and is rather that there are three persons while yet some unity characterizes them so that they are said to be one, the question that presses is that of the kinds of relation that obtain between them. It is not surprising then that in his significant paper 'Trinity and Ontology', Professor Rowan Williams begins with the issue of the logic of relations.[26] Though I want to discuss this somewhat I think it would be useful to begin with a reminder that modern logic distinguishes between logical forms. Though the notion of an argument is by no means either simple or univocal it is easily enough grasped and we can readily agree that logic is concerned with argument. In the elementary logic we may have been taught we may then simply have talked of propositions as the elements of argument and terms as the elements of propositions. However, the modern logician is interested in the fact that each sentence or proposition that makes up an argument has the character being either true or false – whether they are known to be so or not they are the kinds of sentences that could be true (and so could be

---

[25] Ibid., 28, 3 ad 1.
[26] Rowan Williams, 'Trinity and Ontology', in Kenneth Surin (ed.), *Christ, Ethics and Tragedy, Essays in Honour of Donald MacKinnon*, Cambridge: Cambridge University Press 1989, pp. 71–92.

false). I think it is also important to note in passing that when
the sentence is part of an argument it asserts that something is
the case – that is, it makes a factual claim. The distinction that
is then made is between sentential logical form and predicate
logical form. The importance of this is that when what two sentences state cannot be dissociated, when, that is, roughly speaking they say the same thing, then the same symbol is used to
denote each sentence when we abstract the form – and form, after
all, is the main interest of logic. Thus 'Brutus killed Caesar' and
'Caesar was killed by Brutus' are not identical in grammatical
form, something which would be very important for the translation of these sentences into some language other than English.
Yet what is asserted by either is the same as the other.

This may not seem to help us very much in understanding
Trinitarian doctrine; but it will at least show that 'God is the
Father of the Lord Jesus Christ' and 'The Lord Jesus Christ is the
Son of God' can be seen as correlative sentences whatever view
we take of the debate between realism and idealism. We shall
come back to the problem of relations and I hope that this distinction will help us clarify that issue. However, let me conclude
this brief exposition of logical form. Predicate logic refines and
develops traditional grammatical analysis of sentences into subject and predicate. It looks for common names and common predicate in the sentences composing an argument which indicate
their dependence. Any further discussion of the distinction would
complicate matters without any benefit. So let me try to illustrate the relevance and utility of this distinction. In the
Institutes (Book I, chapter xiii) Calvin comments of the position
of Sabellius thus: 'When the matter was debated, he acknowledged his belief that the Father was God, the Son God, the
Spirit God; but then he had the evasion ready, that he had said
nothing more than if he had called God powerful, and just and
wise.' Whether Calvin was right in what he said about
Sabellius or about what happens in Trinitarian doctrine he
clearly saw there was a fundamental logical difference between
the two sets of statements. His view of Sabellius is that he was
confused and inconsistent. It was to meet the threat of such false
doctrine, he thought, that the word *persona* was in fact introduced. What Calvin grasped was that the Trinitarian doctrine
was concerned to make assertions which could be taken as making
the same truth-claim – 'God is Father Son and Spirit' and 'The

three persons are one substance'. By contrast Sabellius, he thought, was making predications of God which could not have that relation. I referred earlier to the traditional Aristotelian division of propositions into 'terms', the subject and predicate (vide *Prior Analytics* and *De Interpretatione*). So it was Predicate logic which interested him. If we consider the development of this in modern logic it might help clarify matters. Modern logicians refer to the predicate as an operator or function. This notion of function can be understood if we take the two sentences 'Ardbeg is the finest Malt Whisky' and 'I believe that Ardbeg is the finest Malt Whisky'. The second is derived from the first by the addition of the truth-operator 'I believe that . . .'. It is then known as a function of the first. So a proposition constructed from a name by the addition of a predicate may be called the function of its subject. The subject is the argument of either the function or of the predicate.

I have referred to this distinction between logical forms for two reasons. The first is the important consideration that Logic is essentially a formal study so that there is a natural tendency to be impatient with it because we feel that the whole discussion is abstract. It lacks that intimacy of concern with matters that move us. The reaction is what Aneurin Bevan expressed in his acid description of Hugh Gaitskell as 'a desiccated calculating-machine'. However, it is the very formalism of logic that enabled it to be so powerful a tool in the hands of men like Anselm who have created theology for us. If it does not matter whether you are talking of apples, pears or onions when you are doing logic then is it not likely to be exactly the tool you need in the difficult task of theology? Secondly, this has been a useful way of bringing out the very problem we mentioned as the central logical problem in Trinitarianism, that of relations. Predicate logic's analysis of positions like Sabellius' reveals why it is that they will not work – it is precisely that there is no relation involved in the assertion they make.

Let me now turn to Professor Williams' paper. He devotes much space and argument at the beginning to the ontology he thinks MacKinnon builds on Moore's refutation of Bradleian idealism. By refuting Bradley's argument that there can be no external relations, says MacKinnon,[27] Moore establishes 'something about the world', 'a fact of a peculiar order'. Professor Williams complains about this language that it is unhelpful if not indeed unintelligible. He thinks that what Moore is doing is stipulating an ontological framework, defining what facts are. 'If p and q can, independently of each other, be known to be true, they are known to be contingently true' (ibid.). Now that seems to me a singularly odd claim. I can know quite independently that bachelors are unmarried and that $1 + 1 = 2$; but quite clearly neither of these statements is contingently true, both of them being a priori and analytic. Moreover, it will not help us to clarify the relevance of this realist stance of MacKinnon's by saying, as Professor Williams does,[28] that he tends to elide various kinds of antirealism. The whole point, it seems to me, is that for MacKinnon – as indeed he tells us in Borderlands of Theology [29] – the logical work of Moore and Russell was in a peculiar way a preamble to faith. Now it is worth noting that we are talking here of logical work rather than of some general philosophical position. Further MacKinnon says specifically of Moore that it was as much his analysis of perception as a finding as Moore's clear distinction between concept and reality that enabled him, MacKinnon, to be a realist.[30] True, contingency is of fundamental importance in his analysis of Christian language as when he says[31] that the sheer contingency of Christ gives an entirely new use to this logical ontological notion. Here, however, what is relevant and vital is the point of factuality. It reminds me of my own perception of the difference between the Unitarianism I met in England and that which I had known in Wales. The latter was very much an ethical Socinianism whereas the former was much more ready to accept Trinitarian formulations at the price of evacuating their factual claim.

It is not my intention to follow Professor Williams' painstaking, comprehensive and illuminating analysis of both the ontological motifs that form the idiom of MacKinnon's theological writing and his various discussions of the theme of the Trinity. There is one thing, though, which I think he misses – that

[27] Williams, ibid., p. 73.
[28] Ibid., p. 74.
[29] Ibid., pp. 62–5.
[30] Ibid., p. 63.
[31] Ibid., p. 81.

MacKinnon spends more time talking of the Incarnation and of Christology than he does actually discussing the Trinity or elaborating any Trinitarian doctrine. This is an important point to which we shall need to return; but for the moment I want to stay with the logical issues. My first point is that if we are concerned with the problem of internal relations in the language about the Trinity then, despite the fact that Professor Williams is so concerned with the significance of the doctrine of the Holy Spirit, this does only concern the first two persons. This does seem rather an obvious point and perhaps all that I can achieve here is to point out the obvious. It certainly is worth noting both because it reveals the ambiguity of talk about relation and because it has rather puzzling implications. The point is this: that the assertion of internal relations is necessarily true. If then only the relation of the Father and the Son is necessary in what sense is the relation of either to the Spirit accidental since it is asserted that there is an identity of Father, Son and Spirit? I do not think it can be accidental though I am equally clear that the relation is an external one. It is perhaps worth emphasizing that I am using the word 'external' here in the strict logical sense of a relation that is not reversible. The three naming expressions as logicians would call them refer to an identity. It was this which Calvin was pointing to in his reference to the historical necessity of adopting the term *persona*. As he says (*Institutes*, Book I, chapter xiii), when we use the term 'God' we mean to refer to all three persons. Again, he insists on the identity of this assertion with the revelation of Scripture, saying (ibid. 5) that to speak of a Trinity of persons in the one essence of God is to say in one dictum what the Scriptures say. The identity of the three persons is, then a logical identity in so far as there is reference to a single ontological nature, the essence. This seems to bring us to some kind of impasse or even contradiction. One possible solution is the use of the logical notions of definitions and functional equivalent. In *Principia Mathematica* Russell spoke of defined functional equivalence between terms or between propositions, using the sign of a triple parallel line as distinct from the double one of an equal sign. So p is equivalent to q when p if and only if q. That is, p and q have the same truth-value or the same syntactical value in the logical system. It was a similar technique that Anselm had used in his development of Boethian modal logic for the purpose of his arguments about the existence of God – some propositions and terms could be substituted for one another in some circumstances as signifying the same thing.[32]

In his debate with Roscelin, Anselm encountered a similar problem to the one just mentioned. In *De Incarnatione Verbi* he says that if, as Roscelin had been saying, God is one and the same through and through then Father, Son and Holy Spirit are all one person and Roscelin is saying that nothing is proper to any one person. This means that there can be no relation in God and that would make any talk of Father, Son and Spirit quite absurd. His demonstration of the absurdities, he says,[33] may suggest to Roscelin that this is what proves Roscelin's own point; but Anselm rejects the charge that he is compounding not solving difficulties, arguing that God is the Highest God and in that we cannot conceive of plurality of *substantia* or *essentia*.[34] It is in exactly the same way that centuries later Calvin spoke of the 'the simple unity of God'[35] and 'the simple unity of essence'.[36]

This rather involved argument about the place of internal relation in the doctrine of the Trinity makes it clear, I think, that there are two very different poles to Trinitarian theology – the empirical and the metaphysical. It may perhaps be said that this is a lot of fuss for next to nothing. As I have said before, it is the obvious that I grasp. However, it is not less important a point for being obvious that Trinitarian theology begins from the conviction that God has revealed himself in Jesus Christ and that it goes on to say that this was, as Acts says, a beginning. To discuss what we mean by 'God' in this context is otiose because it is quite clear that the notion is not merely the legacy of the O.T. religion with its massive insistence on the unity and singularity of God who is Yahweh. It is also the notion shaped by the philo-sophical refinement of Greek mythology. I complained as loudly as most and more insistently than many when Tillich spoke sim-ply of an identity of the Biblical God and the Absolute Being of Philosophy; but this far I have always and still am prepared to go with him. You cannot have Christian doctrine without the involvement of Greek metaphysics. The starting-point of a Trini-tarian theology, then, must be the clarification of what is in-

---

[32] Henry, op. cit., n. 9 above.
[33] Anselm, *De Incarnatione Verbi* S. 2, 20, 6–7.
[34] Ibid., S. 2, 23, 3-4.
[35] John Calvin, *Institutes of the Christian Religion*, I, xiii, 29.
[36] Ibid., 23f.

volved in this confession of Jesus Christ as Lord. I say 'involved in' quite deliberately rather than 'implied by' for there are two kinds of involvement here which are more important than the implications of that confession.

First, it seems to me that any Christology worth having is an attempt to speak of that indissoluble relation of God and Christ of which the Fourth Gospel is so marvellous and dramatic a presentation. Again and again I come back to Chapter 14 with its simple categorical propositions – 'I and the Father are one', 'Whoever has seen me has seen the Father'. It is unthinkable that the writer did not understand what was being said here about relation. Yet half the theological point as the major part of the dramatic effect (or dramatic irony as Bultmann would say) lies in the context – that is, in the tragic end of Jesus' ministry and the apparent failure so powerfully described by Schweitzer long ago. This is where I am so impressed by Professor Williams' careful delineation of the tragic element, indeed 'the tragic sense of life' as Unamuno's Kierkegaardian phrase puts it. I will not try to rival that and say no more about it beyond two simple points. First, whatever we say God is, there is a sense in which he is clearly and necessarily the answer to the problems posed by the human predicament. Secondly – and this is more important – the human situation is not some starting point which is then abandoned: it is the door to our understanding of the nature of reality. So, then, I insist that any real Christology has the task, in Donald MacKinnon's words, 'of reconciling the use of the category of substance in the articulation of the christological problem with the recognition that it is the notion of kenosis which more than any other single notion points to the deepest sense of the mystery of the incarnation'.[37]

The second reason why I speak of 'involved in' rather than of implication is that I want to refer to the presuppositions of Christology. I have always maintained that without a doctrine of creation a Christology is impossible. Many years ago my friend Arnold Ehrhardt of revered memory, published a paper in *Studia Theologica* (later reprinted in his *Framework of the New*

---

[37] '"Substance" in Christology: A Cross-bench view' in S. W. Sykes and J. P. Clayton (eds.), *Christ, Faith and History: Cambridge Studies in Christology,* Cambridge University Press 1972, pp. 279–300 (p. 297).

Testament Stories)[38] on *creatio ex nihilo.* He concluded by saying that the world was created at the Resurrection of Christ. He was faithfully articulating the christocentric doctrine of creation outlined by his mentor Karl Barth. Many of these points I am very happy to acknowledge and maintain. However, to maintain that there is an ontological identity between creation and resurrection is a disastrous mistake if not indeed nonsense. Clearly it is not the simple nonsense of saying that the beginning of the play is the third act; but it is disastrous inasmuch as there is no possibility of speaking about God raising Christ from the dead unless we have articulated a doctrine of God as Creator which is our warrant for speaking of a world and his action in it.

Once more I return to that sophisticated theologian, Calvin; for this was a point he grasped very clearly. I know that several scholars have insisted that there is no natural theology in Calvin and I do not dispute that for him all God's work is revealed in Christ in so far as it is in his face that we see all those comfortable truths of our salvation, including predestination. Yet I defy anyone to read the opening chapters of the *Institutes* and not agree that for Calvin the creation is logically distinct from and prior to our salvation. For our purpose here the most interesting example is the complicated discussion of the position of the Father in the Trinity. With his customary honesty and impatience with reductionist clarity he admits that he finds himself perplexed at points; but he nevertheless insists that the Father is the principium of the Godhead.[39]

Before concluding this paper I must return to the problem of relations and try to clarify the ontological implications of what I have said by referring to properties. Surely, as we saw when looking as St Thomas' discussion, one of the most difficult things in talking of the Trinity is describing the relations. To my mind so much of traditional discussion of 'relation' and 'person' is verbal or semantic and thus a great deal of it is confused. I am sure that traditional opposition to Trinitarianism is in part at least derived from a confusion about the relations. When the critic says that there are only relations the orthodox theologian replies that this is wrong because there are three subsistents. To

[38] Arnold Ehrhardt, *The Framework of the New Testament Stories,* Manchester 1964.
[39] John Calvin, ibid., I, xiii, 18, 20, 24 and 26.

which the critic then replies that if there are three persons then this is, to quote Matthew Arnold, like talking of three Lord Shaftesburies. However, if we say that the Father has to the Trinity the relation which is that He is one of this group of three then we could also say that the Son and the Spirit also have the same relation to the group, and this is the kind of problem that confuses our discussion of St Thomas' language. This is, however, a mistake because there is in strict logic no relation which can be so described. That the Father is a member of this group of three is a fact and the relation of the Father to the group does not consist in that fact – which is why I was so anxious to reject Professor Williams' criticism of MacKinnon's talk of facts earlier.

To return to the question of the relation of the Father to the group, the relation that He has is that of being a member of the group and that bare logical definition is something which can be said of each of the other two. Father, Son and Spirit are each a member of that group in precisely the same sense. Hence it was that Calvin could quite properly speak of the indefinite use of the term 'God' as referring to any or all of the Trinity. But that presupposes the difference between relation and fact now made. The point is that there could not be that identity of relation if the relation consisted in the fact that the Father is a member of the group. I think it is worth emphasizing here that in dealing with matters of logic we are dealing with abstract form. One reason why this is important is that unless we remember this we shall expect the artificiality of logic, if I may so describe the abstraction, to conform to the naturalness of ordinary language – in this case that of devotion. Another reason is that precisely because we abstract from the truth that the Father is a member of this group of three we are not talking about the truth as such but only an element of it. An abstract painting can refer to a building but will represent only an element of it. The element of the Trinity as an abstraction is something that can be maintained of all three indiscriminately.

Having mentioned Calvin let me now say that for this reason I am not so impressed either by the usual criticism of St Thomas, viz., that he confused relations and properties. But whether he did or not the fact of the matter is that relations are constituents or elements of properties though they are not identical with properties. To continue with the point about the membership of the Trinity we can distinguish the relation the Father, Son and Spirit independently have to the Trinity from the property of having this relation which belongs to all three. Clearly as far as Trinitarian doctrine is concerned the most important point is to distinguish between the kinds of properties described as having a relation – in particular between having a relation to someone or other of a group of things which is neither the relation to any particular one not that to the group as such. I am one father's son and not the son of a group of fathers. In saying that I am not saying that I am my particular father's son. The property is something characteristic of all men.

My concern throughout this discussion is to show how logic is both distant from reality and yet brings us to issues of ontology. In short, I have been concerned with finding ways of talking of the reality of the three persons of the Trinity. All of us are familiar with the logical dogma that existence is not a property but I imagine most of us talk of things having the property of being real. Thus we distinguish between the character of Mr Micawber in David Copperfield and Mr Dickens senior, Charles' father on whom this character was modelled; and we could say that Dickens had the property of being real. Now there is no question about the vivid credibility of the picture in David Copperfield – the man who instructs young David in the art of financial management but whose constant confidence is that 'something will turn up' lives before our mind's eye as we read. The description Dickens offers us is so brilliantly observant and graphic that Micawber cannot be taken for Mr Dick or (pardoning the pun) for any other Tom, Dick or Harry. It is obvious, however, that Dickens was of all novelists the most autobiographical and indeed could be said to have always written his own life. Obvious too is the fact that Charles Dickens had the property of being his father's son and that this was part of that extraordinary biography which was the reality of Dickens. In other words, Dickens senior affected the life of Charles, produced changes in it which we know.

I am not trying to devise some analogy with Scripture but simply wanting to make a point about the reality of experience; for it is the reality of Christian experience from which the postulation of a Trinity is made. Very important clearly is the trinitarian rather than the binitarian nature of the postulate. This is where it seems to me that the ontological concern we have uncovered makes us particularly aware of the difficulty of grasping the mystery of God's presence in Christ. What I have in mind is that from what I have said so far about the origin of the doctrine of the Trinity it might be thought that a binitarian scheme should serve us equally well. But the greatest mystery is God's presence in Christ on the cross in his dying and in his death. Strangely enough I think this is where talk about substance is in fact inevitable. Merely to consider the different emphases of the Gospels is to be led to an appreciation of that difficulty I mentioned: one thinks of the contrast between Luke's and John's portrayals of Christ's victory. But that is a small contrast when one thinks of the variety of Christian devotion and also considers the very different expressions of them in Puritan poetry and that of some twentieth century poets like R. S. Thomas and again of Bach's Passions and the very different world of Mozart's *Requiem*. Yet in all this what I find most striking is the unity of the believer's confidence. This seems worlds away from talk about substance; but I do contend that it is precisely such a perception that is the impulse to the language of substance. I think again of that man of faith and commentator on the Scriptures, Calvin, with his unhesitating use of the words essence and substance. This might be thought unnecessarily old-fashioned; but if we recall that theology has the task of identifying God then it may show that this is neither wrong nor useless talk. Elijah was no philosopher of religion but his encounter with the prophets of Baal gives philosophy of religion rich matter for thought. The question was quite simply to distinguish between two gods. If two things are distinguished as discernibly different then we say that they are different things – Mr Micawber is not Mr Dick. If, however, two things are strictly indiscernible then we will say that they are identical, are one thing. It was to express that identity that the Fathers used the language of substance in talking of God. That identity distinguishes the completeness of the victory as John records it and it distinguishes too the completeness of the fulfilled promise as Acts relates the story of the young church. This is why the Trinitarian scheme was necessary. A binitarian one would make only a christological point and a faulty one at that. The three modalities of time are here involved and there are three persons presupposed.

In conclusion I want to go back to what I said about human existence as the door to our understanding of reality. It is death that represents the key to that door – not because we would say with Heidegger that we beings facing death or existing for death but rather because, as we recall Wittgenstein said, death is not an event in life. Though it is indeed not something I live through it is the property common to all human experience. That this is, though obvious, far from trivial is clear if we listen to that theological giant among the Romantics, John Keats. As a young man already aware because of his medical training that his was a borrowed time he penned those immortal lines:

When I have fears that I may cease to be
Before my pen has gleaned my teeming brain
. . . then on the shore
Of the wide world I stand alone, and think
Till love and fame to nothingness do sink.

Love and fame – yes, even that completeness – sink to nothingness, he says. The other side of that solitary ontological shock is Dylan Thomas' great refrain in his poem 'Death shall have no dominion' which ends with the confident assertion – 'And death shall have no more dominion'. What this poetry reveals to us is not just the ontological fact that here is a property we all share 'born to die', as Dylan's Eli Jenkins puts it – but also the ontological truth that death is transcended. The reason why I quoted Keats' poem is that there is here a Trinitarian structure. His brain and his pen were what life had given him and 'creature of the fleeting hour' was the so ephemeral present of his experience. But beyond the nothingness to which all sank was the mystery of death itself and that mysterious future of which Dylan speaks so eloquently. Ontology thus is a beginning as well as the end of Trinitarian logic of relations.

4. Art: A Trinitarian Imperative?

Brian L. Horne

In 1956 Michael Tippett gave a talk broadcast by the BBC in which he addressed the question of the nature of the artistic creation:

> The drive to create has been so constant through the ages, and is so intense in its operation, that it is difficult for those submitting to it not to feel it is evidence of things beyond the individually personal. I believe the faculty the artist may sometimes have to create images through which the mysterious depths of our being speak to us, is a true fundamental. I believe it is part of what we mean by having knowledge of God.[1]

In the thirty-four years which have passed, Tippett has shown no sign of departing from this view of the impulse to create as being, in some way, ineluctably religious – however problematic that term may be and however difficult it has been to maintain such a position in a relentlessly secularizing culture. The attempt to sever the connection between the realm of art and that of the sacred has been, at the level of philosophical theory, so constant a pressure in Western European society from the beginning of the eighteenth century that it has become somewhat trite to point out the fact. From time to time voices have been raised against this severance, notably Coleridge's and Ruskin's in the nineteenth century and T. S. Eliot and Allen Tate in our own; but the history of that branch of philosophy we call aesthetics in the past two centuries offers few examples of philosophers or critics (I do not speak of artists themselves who, like Tippett frequently seem conscious of a religious dimension) who have been prepared to ground their concept of the beautiful and their theory of art in the notion of a divine reality.

In the last decade, however, the radically non-religious aesthetics of most contemporary critical theorizing have been questioned by two thinkers of whom one, ironically, specifically disclaimed any belief in God; and the other who has preferred to

---

[1] Anthony Sellars, reviewing Tippett's *New Year*, in *Opera Now*, June 1990.

leave the question of his personal belief unanswered. It is with the thoughts of these two that I should like to begin.

Two months before his death on 28 April 1990 the art critic Peter Fuller wrote a new Foreword to his collection of essays *Images of God. The Consolation of Lost Illusions* originally published in 1985.[2] In it he confirmed unambiguously a tendency in his thought about the nature and purpose of art which had been growing in the years since the book's first appearance:

> For myself, I remain an incorrigible atheist; that is my proclamation of faith. But there is something about the experience of art, itself, which compels me to reintroduce the category of the 'spiritual'. More than that, I believe that, given the ever-present absence of God, art, and the gamut of aesthetic experience, provides the sole remaining glimmer of transcendence. The best we can hope for is that aesthetic surrogate for salvation; redemption through form. (p. xiv)

It is not easy (perhaps it is impossible) to know what precise and meaningful content can be given to the concluding phrase 'redemption through form', though it is redolent with a specific religious interpretation. But we shall leave that aside for the moment and note only the attempt to relocate the production of, and the response to, the artefact in a world in which the *lingua franca* is not that of religious experience. This necessity had already been adumbrated in the short essay of 1983: 'Prophecy and Vision':

> I believe a debate about the spiritual in art is long overdue. Indeed, in all that chatter about the political and social dimensions of art which went on during the last fifteen years, very little attention was paid to what, after all, must be seen as among the most central of all questions affecting art and craft in our century: the severance of arts from religious tradition . . . Modernist art historians tend to regard this as unproblematic . . . But . . . I believe it to be a moot point whether art can ever thrive outside that sort of living, symbolic order, with deep tendrils in communal life, which, it seems, a flourishing religion alone can provide. (p. 189)

The speculations merely sketched in these earlier essays are propounded at far greater length in his last book *Theoria. Art and the Absence of Grace.*[3] It takes the form of an extended and sympathetic critique of John Ruskin whom Fuller 'reads' as the embodiment of the concept of the lost illusion. Again his critical concern in examining both the nature of art at the service of a

---

2 London: Chatto & Windus 1985.
3 London: Chatto & Windus 1989.

particular political ideology with its unique doctrine of man and history, the creative act and the response to that which is created is the paradoxical nature of the transcendental, that is to say the religious dimension. He quotes an essay published by P. T. Forsyth in 1889, *Religion in Recent Art*. The essay itself is a fascinating one and bears directly upon our subject *'Art: A Trinitarian Imperative?'* Forsyth writes: 'The possibility of Art ... depends on a people's idea of God ... Art depends on Religion ... Our religion depends on thought of God. One way of thinking about God makes Art impossible, another makes it inevitable' (pp. 154–5).

It is that concept of inevitability that I am trying to investigate here. What makes art inevitable in human culture? It is not a question that Fuller answers, or, perhaps, that Fuller can answer, given the terms in which he has set up the framework of his own aesthetic, for there is something certainly paradoxical, perhaps even self-contradictory about that aesthetic. He disputes the Marxist view of art (to which he had, himself earlier in life adhered), nor can he agree with Tolstoy, who in *What is Art?* (1898) had famously argued for the necessity of art on the grounds that it was useful as 'a means of union among men, joining them together in the same feelings, and indispensable for the life and progress towards well-being of individuals and humanity'. Fuller examines Ruskin's early view of art that it was revelatory of divinity in that it conveyed the immanence of the divine in the natural world, and traces Ruskin's gradual move away from this notion, based upon what Fuller calls 'natural theology', to a state of disillusionment. And it is on a variation of this that he himself firmly settles: the problematic notion of art as that which invokes and provides the necessary illusion.

This is not a new concept (though Fuller's way of framing it is unique); it is found in this century, for example in the writings of Theodor Adorno and is discussed by Hans Küng in a small book *Art and the Question of Meaning*.[4] He quotes Adorno's cryptic assertion 'Even before Auschwitz, in face of historical experiences, it was an affirmative lie to ascribe to existence any meaning at all (which might have had) consequences even for the form of the work of art' (p. 31). The point being made is that

---

[4] London: SCM Press 1981.

a work of art provides the possibility of defining the meaningless in such a way that it gives the appearance (the affirmative lie) of inward form or 'harmoniousness'. We are not so very far removed from Aristotle's essay on tragedy in *Poetics* in which he argues that the form of the drama enables us not only to consider acts of horror which would be unbearable in real life but to consider them with equanimity and be released from their debilitating dread. Where Adorno differs is that whatever meaning we may attach to a work of art we must acknowledge that the meaning is enclosed in the form and is peculiar to the form and that art is not something which has captured a meaning from the world outside. The relationship between the art-work and the world outside it is at best ambiguous. Needless to say, Küng while sympathetic to the pessimism of Adorno is concerned to show that the world itself has meaning and that works of art are attempts in colour, line, words, movement, sound to grasp and convey that meaning 'without superficial optimism, without any affirmative lie; therefore, instead of a basic mistrust, there can be a *basic trust*. And he (the artist) can give expression to this basic trust in art . . . ' (p. 32) but nevertheless, Küng does not ultimately persuade us (perhaps it was not his intention) of the necessity of art. We are given art as elevating, art as stimulus, art as encouragement, art as revelation; but not (and this is my concern) art as necessity for human existence: art as inevitable.

And so we turn to the second of the two thinkers I mentioned at the beginning of this paper: George Steiner who, throughout his career, has argued for the necessity and inevitability of art in human culture. He returns to the theme in his most recent book *Real Presences*[5] (the book is referred to by Fuller in his new foreword to *Images of God*). His attack upon what Fuller called 'modernism' is not dissimilar from Fuller's and his conclusions are not all that far removed from Fuller's and are equally paradoxical, but his presentation is far subtler and more searching. His familiarity with the language of theology is greater, and he makes extensive use of that language in the crucial parts of his argument. He says quite openly that we are faced with what can only be called theological questions when we are asked to penetrate and elucidate, if we can, the mystery

---

[5] University of Chicago Press 1989.

of artistic creation. He argues for the presence (hence the title of the book) in all art of 'otherness', 'transcendence'. And so he writes:

> The ascription of beauty to truth and to meaning is either a rhetorical flourish or it is a piece of theology. It is a theology explicit or suppressed, masked or avowed, substantive or imagined, which underwrites the presumption of creativity, of signification in our encounters with text, with music, with art. The meaning of meaning is a transcendent postulate. (p. 216)

And when pressed into answering the question why should there be art he answers in terms that have their origin in theological metaphysics:

> . . . there is aesthetic creation because there is *creation* (the word is italicized in the text). There is formal construction because we have been made form. (p. 201)

This is not a new concept to theologians (Thomas Aquinas would have argued no differently on this point) but, conventionally, the theologians, at least in the Western Catholic tradition, have based the argument, or perhaps I should say, have extended the argument to include the notion of the image; that the possibility of artistic creation lies in the fact of our being made in the image of God. It is in the activity of the imagination – of bringing into being, by a combination of mental energy and technical skill, shapes, sounds, sentences that had previously no existence – that the individual feels most 'god-like'. It is an experience of release from the constrictions of the self. This transcendental experience gives content to the belief that man is made in the image of God. I am not arguing that it *exhausts* the content, I am simply remarking on its peculiar power and meaning; and saying that it is of particular significance for us as we consider the human being's capacity to create 'secondary worlds' by art and craft. It implies that the human being is *necessarily* a creator, that art (from the child daubing with a paint brush to a composer producing a symphony) is no luxury to be enjoyed only when the human race has time for the indulgence of such ephemeral pleasures; but is essential to human being.

Paradoxically, though, artistic creation has the appearance of gratuitousness. The human race, as a species, need not create works of art in order to survive; we could remain imaginatively passive and 'dumb' in the world we have been given. It is obvious that painting, dancing, poetry, music are not essential to existence in the way that eating, drinking, sleeping, copulating are. But it is precisely here, at this point of apparent gratuitousness, that the human being becomes human and is distinguished from the rest of the created order. There is a radical and unique freedom here. It seems that the human can choose not to create – and still remain in life. This brings us back to George Steiner who has understood something of profound theological and psychological importance when he argues for the necessity of art; for the concept of freedom is central to his argument. He constructs an anthropological aesthetic with the idea of freedom at its base:

> Where seriousness meets with seriousness, exigence with exigence, in the ontological and ethical spaces of the disinterested, where art and practice, imperatively contingent in their own coming into being and intelligible form, meet the receptive potential of a free spirit, there takes place the nearest we can know of the existential realisation of freedom.

And:

> Only in the aesthetic is there the absolute freedom 'not to have come into being'. Paradoxically, it is that possibility of absence which gives autonomous force to the presence of the work.

And with those words 'absolute freedom' Steiner reveals that, for all his use of theological categories of otherness and transcendence, of real presences, he chooses not to move into the realm of theology but remain within the realm of anthropology and yet, nevertheless to stay with the paradox put, as we have already seen, by Peter Fuller; that we must live and move and have our being 'as if' there were some transcendent reality and that art creates the necessary illusion of that reality. We know, and this is what I deduce from Steiner's position, we know that there is no transcendent reality because we possess 'absolute freedom'; the power not to create.

This is where the theologian questions and contradicts with a contradiction that will have farreaching consequences for the theory of art: its genesis and its purpose. The argument is contradicted by the assertion that God alone possesses absolute freedom; He is the transcendent reality who has the power and freedom not to create. His creature, on the other hand, the human being, by contrast and logical definition possesses only relative freedom and is subject to the necessity of creation. Not to do so would be to refuse the conditions of his very being – to pretend to an absolute freedom. Our impulse to creation, to the construction of 'secondary worlds', arises out of our status as creatures endowed with relative freedom.

I have, as yet, said nothing about that which is the subject of this whole conference: the Trinity. I turn to that now and begin by making the suggestion that Peter Fuller's and George Steiner's theories of art remain, at best, paradoxical, and at worst, intellectually dubious – lacking in logical coherence because they are operating, in all their theological language, with a concept of God as undifferentiated Being. And I suggest that the resolution of the contradictions in their positions can only be achieved when the concept of the Trinity is invoked. The theological terms which proliferate in their texts are without specific reference. Their apprehension of what Divinity may or may not be is essentially unitarian and therefore creates what I believe are inseparable problems for bringing about what their theories of art seek: the reconciliation of transcendence and immanence. A unitarian concept of God, that is, God as some kind of undifferentiated transcendent reality, cannot provide the model for the 'real presence' that Steiner argues for in the work of art or guarantee the kind of 'revelation' that Fuller seems to expect a work of art to provide. The freedom and relatedness which Steiner seems to place so centrally in both initial creativity and consequent response (he talks of *cortesia)* is already inherent in the classical concept of the Trinitarian life of God which is recognized as the fundamentally dogmatic structure if one is to make sense of the act of incarnation.

In the making of a work of art the human being exercises a peculiar kind of mental and emotional energy. It is a drive to externalize; a compulsion to express, to symbolize, to embody in material form the visions of the interior eye. This energetic expression is nothing less than the reflection of the divine life of the Trinity. As we consider the meaning of the statement that we are made in the image of God it becomes apparent that the image is not merely that of a God in a unitarian/monotheistic religion, not even the image of the Creator/Father God of the Old Testament (Steiner sometimes suggests that this is what he understands by Divinity). The revelation of Christ: incarnation: a life lived by the Son of God in the power of the Spirit, is the revelation of exchanged love, absolute relatedness and creative energy within the Godhead himself. The image in which we are created and understand ourselves refers back to a life in which there is the eternal self-expression of the Father in His Son or Word and the eternal self-knowledge received in the flowing out and returning of the Spirit. In the human being there is this same drive to move out of the self in order to find the self, the compulsion to self-expression and self-knowledge. This is at the basis of all art.

At the risk of speaking crudely and anthropomorphically, I would say, that just as the human being remains ignorant and unhoused indeed, mute without that explosion of energy we call art, so in God, the Father remains unknowing and mute until he has expressed Himself in His Word. Here is Jacques Maritain's comment on his essay on Art in his book on scholastic aesthetics:

> Here again we can discover in our Art as it were a trace of the Blessed Trinity. *The Word*, says Augustine, *is in a way the art of Almighty God*. And by the Word the whole divine work was done, *omnia per ipsum facta sunt*. It is through His Word and His art that God attains, controls and realises *(rendre compte)* everything He does. *(Art and Scholasticism*, 1933, p. 132)

So artistic creation is possible not merely, as Steiner, following the precepts of many before him, suggests because there is 'creation': an original act of bringing into being, but because there is creation by a Triune God who gives a particular shape to that which He brings into being; a shape which is related to His own Triune nature; a shape which imposes observable and definable conditions upon the creatures so brought into being. In extending his argument that there is art because there is 'creation', Steiner draws our attention to the Hebraic notion that 'God is capable of all speech-acts except that of monologue.' It is this, he says, which 'has generated our acts of reply, of question and counter-question. After the book of Job and Euripides' *Bacchae* there had to be, if man was to bear his being, the means of dialogue with God which are spelt out in our poetics, music and art' (p. 225).

This Hebraic notion of dialogue with the Creator – a kind of absolute freedom to answer back – is, however, as far as the Christian is concerned, superseded by the notion of a dialogue which – if the term may be permitted – precedes the original act of creation: a conversation of the persons within God the Trinity. God speaking Himself in His Word and hearing Himself in His

Spirit: expressing Himself in His Son and receiving Himself in His Spirit. It is not by any other than a Trinitarian action that the world is brought into and sustained in being. The answer the creatures make is, like prayer, not so much a reply to God – our dialogue with Him – but a participation in a dialogue which already exists – the eternal conversation of God Himself. The Incarnation of the Son carries the divine expressiveness into the material of the created order where the Spirit is already 'groaning and travailing' in bringing that order to its predestined end.

It is on these theological grounds that I, again, disagree with Steiner in his assertion – fascinating and provocative though it is – that the making of something 'by the poet, artist and . . . by the composer, is *counter*-creation' (p. 203). He writes 'it is radically agonistic. It is rival. In all substantive art-acts there beats an angry gaiety . . . The human maker rages at his coming-after at being, forever, second to the original and originating mystery of the forming of form' (p. 204). It is the unwillingness to recognize the possibility of the divine mystery as (I use Steiner's word) radically immanent, the Holy Spirit, as well as ultimately transcendent, the Father, and the union of these two modes of Being in the expressive form of the Incarnate Son, that projects this formulation of the artistic creation – as counter-creation; the work itself constituting a rival world. The problem is that, given this presupposition, the possibility of constructing a logically coherent theoretical basis for the cause he wants to plead, namely that of the 'real presence', recedes even further. If human beings are possessed of absolute freedom, this can only issue in the construction of counter-worlds – without 'real presence'. On the other hand, the relative freedom of the human being which is central to the anthropology of the theist issues in the construction of secondary worlds which are potentially significant expressions, not only of the many facets of the human condition but also metaphors of the divine will and expressive of the divine radiance.

It is interesting to observe P. T. Forsyth adumbrating, but not developing, a similar argument in that essay of 1889 when he points out that 'A distant God, an external God, who from time to time, interferes in Nature or the soul, is not a God compatible with Art', nor he adds tartly, are these images of God 'good for piety'. His complaint against the British art of his own day chimed with his criticism of Anglo-Saxon religion as being 'imperfectly Christianised as yet by the principle of Incarnation' (p. 156). Whether he was correct in so characterizing Anglo-Saxon religion is a moot point which there is no time to discuss here. What is significant for our purposes is the connection he makes between art and incarnation: a connection which had already been emphasized in B. F. Westcott's essay of only three years earlier: 'The Relation of Christianity to Art' (*Epistles of John*, 1886). It is a connection which has a long history, of course. It is central to the Eastern church's theology of icons: it was the nodal point of the controversy which threatened to divide the church in the seventh and eighth and nineth centuries and is enshrined in the lapidary statements of the Second Council of Nicaea (AD 787).

What is lacking in Forsyth's essay, and also in Westcott's, is any serious consideration of the work of the Holy Spirit. Their eyes are focussed on the christological issue: the fact of the Incarnation. But a theory of art cannot be merely christological; one cannot account for art by pointing to the person of Jesus Christ; an aesthetic cannot be constructed on christological grounds alone. It is characteristic of much modern writing on the subject of art and religion that while the doctrine of the image of God and that of the Incarnation receive extensive treatment, the doctrine of the Spirit receives only passing attention. This same weakness is to be found in Aidan Nichols' extensive study *The Art of God Incarnate*:[6]

> The appearing of a supreme image throws open the way for the creation of a theological art apt to serve as exegesis of this new situation of the embodied disclosure of God in man. If God has elected to show himself definitively in the form of a human life, then may not the artist shape and fashion rival images which will add up to an exegesis of revelation? (p. 48)

True . . . But. The human being can become a presence of God in so far as there is a real presence in the human spirit, embodied as that is in the world, of God's own spirit. What enables the human artwork – poem, symphony, dance, statue, – to become the expressive form of divine radiance is the human will responding freely to the movement of the Holy Spirit. So, I would state that while the argument for the possibility, or potentiality, of

---

[6] London: Darton, Longman & Todd 1980.

artistic creation is lodged in the doctrine of the image (creation); the propriety of artistic creation is lodged in the doctrine of the Incarnation; and the necessity or inevitability of artistic creation is lodged in the doctrine of the Spirit. It is not only that we may, in Nichols' words 'fashion images which will add up to an exegesis of revelation'; it is that we *must* fashion such images if we are to live in, and be obedient to, the Spirit. That this Spirit is the Spirit of the Incarnate Word and Risen Lord is, of course, something I should want to emphasize; but it must seem that it is the Spirit who appropriates and expropriates through human persons, material of creation to bring into being secondary worlds.

There are passages in the last volume of Hans Urs von Balthasar's *The Glory of the Lord* which help to illuminate this argument. It must be acknowledged that human creativity in the sense in which I have been discussing it is not a major concern of Balthasar at this point of his book, but his remarks about the role of the Spirit in apprehending the glory of God and achieving the glorification of man do have a precise bearing upon my subject. In a section dealing with the eschatological hope of Christians, he writes:

> But those who advocate utopia presume that they can become fathers of the future without having been children of the past. They want to create without having received – and that would mean being God himself.[7]

The interesting phrase is 'create without having received'. Of course Balthasar may not have works of art in mind here, but as we transpose this phrase into the key of art we find that the criticism of the utopians becomes applicable to the position of George Steiner. Steiner, of course, would be the last person to claim that the artist can create *ex nihilo* ignorant of the whole immense artistic tradition to which he or she is heir; nevertheless – and in this perhaps lies part of the incoherence of his position – he sees art arising out of an absolute freedom on the part of the human being, and it is the art work itself which is supposed to signify and embody this freedom. My position, as I have tried to show, is quite different: the human being possesses only relative freedom, and the boundaries or shape of that

---

[7] Hans Urs von Balthasar, *The Glory of the Lord. A Theological Aesthetics*, v VII, ed. by John Riches, Eng. trans. by Brian McNeil, Edinburgh: T & T Cla 1989, p. 527.

freedom are determined by the gift of the Spirit. What has been 'received' (to use Balthasar's word) is not merely the past – tradition, history, the form of the world – but the Spirit of God who, alone, moves in total freedom. What drives the world to its eschatological destiny is, in terms of Christian theology, the Spirit. What drives the artist to create (and perhaps all real artistic creations point in some mysterious way to the eschaton) is, similarly, the Spirit.

A few pages earlier in this volume Balthasar has focussed on the work of the Spirit in relation to the Triune glory. 'Since the Spirit himself is the glorification of the love between the Father and the Son, wherein God's true glory disclosed itself to us, it is likewise only he who can bring about glorification in the world.' (p. 389) It would be my contention that the purpose of all art is to participate in the disclosure of God's glory in the world, even the works of art – say for instance, certain plays by Samuel Beckett or paintings by Francis Bacon, which seem only to point to the absence of the glory. They are negative demonstrations of the possibility of glory and achieve their power only because of this unstated but acknowledged possibility. Such works portray the pain and anxiety which arise out of the radical disjunction which is perceived by the artist between what is and what could, or even should, be. So Balthasar writes:

> His [that is, the Spirit's] work unfolds as a consequence of the bringing about of a 'distance' between the Father and the Son in the kenosis and the 'abolition' of this in the return of the Son to the Father. . . . (p. 389)

To talk of the 'spiritual' in art is therefore to talk very precisely, accurately and definitively; it is to refer to the means by which the Spirit's work of revelation and glorification unfolds as a consequence of the 'kenosis' of the Incarnation: a 'distance' in the Godhead, and the 'abolition' of that distance in the Godhead by the Ascension of the one who was 'poured out'. 'The openness of the human to the divine which permits him or her to express the divine is what is most characteristically human in every person' argues Aidan Nichols (p. 133). Since self-expressive energy has been revealed to us as the very structure of the life of God, it cannot be an activity which is optional in the life of creatures who are made in that image: it is a Trinitarian imperative. We may not choose *not* to create if we are to be human.

5. Relation and Relativity: The Trinity and the Created World

Colin E. Gunton

I. Words and the World – Again[1]

Discussion of the relation between the world and the words with which we attempt to describe, characterize or generally come to terms with it are as old as philosophy itself. Plato's proposal presents one clear option: the world, if properly – that is, rationally – approached is found to contain, embodied more or less adequately within its shifting and temporal materiality, the objective and timeless ideas or forms which give it its structure and reality. The mind's task is to discover what they are by thought, by abstraction. They are to be found by reflection on certain of the general words from the vocabulary of thought. Kant's programme contains a second option, and it is an inversion of Plato's. The concepts are, indeed, both timeless and, in a sense, objective. But their *locus* is not reality, 'out there', so much as the structures of human rationality. The human mind replaces exterior eternity as the location of the concepts by means of which reality is understood.

Both proposals, insofar as so crude a summary can begin to do justice to their subtlety, are idealist, and, indeed, systems of transcendental idealism. The difference between them lies in the nature and location of their transcendentality. Plato's ideas are absolutely objective, constituting as they do the eternal structure of the universe. It is therefore a realistic idealism. Kant's concepts are subjectively objective, inhering in the structures of human rationality, and therefore tend to generate a more

---

[1] A previous and differently oriented treatment of this topic is to be found in my *The Actuality of Atonement. A Study of Metaphor, Rationality and the Christian Tradition*, Edinburgh: T & T Clark 1988, ch. 2.

subjective idealism, calling into question the very possibility of our being able to speak in our words of the world as it actually is.

Despite the claims, sometimes heard, that the philosophies of both men, and particularly Plato, have been refuted beyond hope of salvation, there is much to be said for aspects of both systems, and in particular their common quest for transcendentality. May they not both be right in holding that there are concepts without which we cannot make sense of our world – or rather, more positively, that enable us to *think* our world? Put more carefully, may it not be suggested that inherent within certain words there lies the possibility of *conceiving* things as they are? Here, of course, the choice is for aspects of Plato's realistic programme: to seek concepts which are in some way or other rooted in or indicative of the deep structures of reality. At this point, however, one of Kant's objections to the platonic quest must be faced. Does not the history of metaphysical speculation present to us a spectacle of empty battles, battles fought without hope of victory?

The answer to Kant's question is a Yes, but. Yes indeed, but (1) what else is to be expected? Does the propriety of the quest for transcendentals depend on an expectation of the kind of final solutions that Kant rather arrogantly claimed that he had himself found? But (2) even within the inconclusive skirmishing, do we not find a wide general agreement on the kind of concepts we are looking for, even if there is much disagreement on how we are to understand them? The example given by Tom Stoppard's philosopher, George, in opposition to relativistic theories of ethics is as good as any:

> Certainly a tribe which believes it confers honour on its elders by eating them is going to be viewed askance by another which prefers to buy them a little bungalow somewhere, and Professor McFee should not be surprised that the notion of honour should manifest itself so differently in peoples so far removed in clime and culture. What is surely more surprising is that notions such as honour should manifest themselves at all. For what *is* honour?[2]

But that takes us to a further consideration. It is to Hegel and some of those who influenced him that we owe the injection into the debate of a category that played no constitutive part in the thought of either Plato or Kant. It is that of history. If we take

---

2 Tom Stoppard, *Jumpers*, London: Faber 1972, pp. 54f.

the history of thought seriously, we have to concede that such transcendentals as there are can be read timelessly neither off the structure of the world nor from the shape of human rationality. They emerge, rather, in the commerce, the interaction, between the two. There is thus more of a dynamism involved than either of those two philosophers were able, in their place in the history of thought, to incorporate in their philosophy. It requires attention to the fact that the same, or the same kinds of, concepts may appear in different cultural contexts and may be related but not identical in meaning. We shall note examples later in the chapter. It follows that the battles of which Kant was so scornful may not be empty battles at all, but part of the intellectual process. Because combatants are disagreed about some, even many, features of the concepts of God or of beauty, it does not follow that nothing about the way things are can be discovered in the dialectic of ideas.

The fact that the transcendentals emerge in the interaction between mind and world means that neither a straight platonic not a pure Kantian approach to the problem is right. We are rather in the realm of what Sabina Lovibond has called the parochial transcendental, concepts which are not absolutely transcendental in the platonic sense but which in some way or other belong in our embodiedness in the world.[3] The interesting question then becomes not simply which transcendentals are the right ones and so enable us to understand or indwell our world the better, but also how we light upon them at all. We are here close to the questions of revelation and discovery: not of what is known as particular divine revelation, so much of the more universal question of whether things make themselves known to us in such a way that our concepts are not simply constructed by our minds – as the Kantian picture has it – but are a response to something prevenient. But the theological question also raises its head.   Whence come the prevenience and the capacity for response? Where do the concepts come from in the first place?

Let me take as an example a passage, which I have already used in a different though related context, from Michael Faraday's famous paper on electricity and the nature of matter. Faraday's paper is part of the process whereby nineteenth

---

[3] Sabina Lovibond, *Realism and Imagination in Ethics,* University of Minnesota Press 1983, pp. 210ff.

century science moved away from the conception, beloved of
mechanistic atomists, of the universe as a collocation of
mutually impenetrable parts, to a more relativistic notion. He
suggests a concept of atoms as fields of force rather than discrete
substances, and develops a theory of the 'mutual penetrability of
atoms'. His way of putting the matter is remarkable, that
'matter is not merely mutually penetrable, but each atom
extends, so to say, throughout the whole of the solar system, yet
always retaining its own centre of force'.[4] Physics has, of course,
come a long way since then, in extending Faraday's 'solar system'
to the whole of the universe and in the vast extension and
mathematizing of the concepts he suggested. But I begin with
him for a very good reason. He speaks of the solar system rather
as the classical trinitarian theologians did of the Trinity. What
we have in Faraday is a kind of doctrine of the *perichoresis*, the
interpenetration, of matter. As the three persons of the Trinity
interpenetrate the being of the others, so it is with the matter of
which the world is made.

I am not suggesting that the doctrine of the Trinity is in any
way necessarily responsible for the way that Faraday came to
think – at least not directly – although it cannot be denied that
there are theological determinants in many systems of thought,
certainly in modern science, however much it may think that it
has outgrown its parentage.[5] Rather, I want to ask whether
concepts generated by theology, and particularly trinitarian
theology, bear any relation to those employed in conceiving the
world as it is presented to us in some of the discoveries of modern
science. That is to say, I am going to ask some questions about
conceptual similarities, and raise the question of whether the
concepts developed in trinitarian theology enable us not only to
conceive the reality of God, but also have transcendental pos-

---

[4] Michael Faraday, 'A Speculation touching Electric Conduction and the
Nature of Matter', in Richard Laming (ed.), *On the Primary Forces of
Electricity*, 1838, pp. 7f. For a use of Faraday in Christology, see my
Yesterday and Today. A Study of Continuities in Christology, London:
Darton, Longman & Todd 1983, p. 117.
[5] Since first writing that, I have come to learn that the suggestion may not
be so wide of the mark. See Geoffrey Cantor, *Michael Faraday:
Sandemanian and Scientist. A Study of Science and Religion in the
Nineteenth Century*, London: Macmillan 1991, p. 172, suggests that
Faraday's conception of the notion of unity in diversity reveals 'a clear
echo of the Christian tri-unity'.

sibilities, and so enable us to come to terms with the fundamental shape of being.

The question, necessarily involved in such an enquiry, of whether the world is *like* the God conceived to be triune, is an odd and difficult one. Faraday's words suggest that in some respects it is. But if it is taken to suggest that the world is in some way in the image of God, it causes two problems in particular. The first is that it makes it difficult to distinguish between the being of the world and that of the human creature. In avoiding such a difficulty, it must be argued that to be in the image of God is to be personal, and that is the distinctive mark of the human creation over against the rest of the creation. The second, and it is the same point made from a different angle, is that if the being of the world is conceived to be in the image of God – as it undoubtedly is in some systems of metaphysics – it becomes impossible to conceive adequately the character of the non-human creation. Rather, I should want to hold that the distinctive being of the world is what it is in relation to persons, but that it is not itself personal. The pitfalls of personalizing the world are many, and shown by the otherwise interesting attempts of Process philosophers like Hartshorne to use relational language of all dimensions of being. Against that, the thesis to be argued here is that the world is like God not in being in his image, but in the more limited sense that there are some conceptual parallels between the concepts in which the being of God is expressed and the ways in which we may conceive the world. I shall illustrate the parallels by appeal to some modern scientific conceptuality. The claim to be argued is that some trinitarian concepts appear to bear a certain likeness to some of the concepts that have been either appropriated or developed by modern scientists.

II. Outlines of a Trinitarian Theology of Creation

Before, however, I engage directly in that enterprise, I want to outline, as background and support, the basic content of a trinitarian theology of creation. The advantage of a trinitarian approach to the theology of creation is that it enables us to say a number of important things, chief among them that the world is 'good', a distinct reality with its own being, and yet only so by virtue of its dependence upon and directedness to God. The basis of a trinitarian theology of creation was already marked out by Irenaeus in his engagement with the world-denying theologies of his opponents. He argued that because the world was created through the Son, it is real and good; and that because the Son became incarnate, there is a continuity between creation and redemption, between all the will and works of God in and towards the world. It is therefore according to Irenaeus the material world as a whole which is destined for redemption, and indeed already participating in it by virtue of the work of the eschatological Spirit.

Later trinitarian theology enables us to see more clearly the importance of the doctrine of the immanent Trinity. Because God is, 'before' creation took place, already a being-in-relation, there is no *need* for him to create what is other than himself. He does not need to create, because he is already a *taxis*, order, of loving relations. In some recent theology it has been suggested that such a theology is to be rejected on the grounds that, if God does not need the creation in some way or other, he must be a distant and unfeeling monarch. Such an objection confuses two points. The first is the proper objection to the form that doctrines of aseity have sometimes taken, suggesting as they do the total lack of involvement, of an Epicurean kind, of a completely immutable and unfeeling deity. Yet it does not follow that for God to enter into relation with the world he must need it in some way.

And the second point is that far from suggesting an unrelatedness of God to the world, trinitarian theology is based on the belief that God the Father is related to the world through the creating and redeeming action of Son and Spirit who are, in Irenaeus' expression, his two hands. The doctrine of the Trinity, certainly in the form advocated in this paper, is indeed *derived* from the involvement of God in creation, reconciliation and redemption. But what it also enables us to say is that far from being dependent upon the world God is free to create a world which can be itself, that is to say, free according to its own order of being. It is the relation-in-otherness between God and the world that is conceived with the help of the doctrine of the Trinity, and probably cannot adequately be conceived in any other way. The world is itself, not God, but worldly according to its own measure of being. Yet it is so by gift of the God who creates and sustains it in such a way that it is itself.[6]

III. Some Trinitarian Concepts

What, then, are the features of the doctrine of the Trinity of which echoes are to be found in recent scientific thought? A number of them arise out of the discussion of a trinitarian theology of creation in the previous section, but another will need to be added. Central among them are two, the concepts of relation and of freedom. The former has a chequered history. In the Cappadocians, it was developed to be able to speak of the way in which the persons of Father, Son and Spirit are to each other. The relation of Father and Son was centrally expressed by means of an analogy from human reproduction, in terms of begetting; that between Father and Spirit in the distinct but more vague and less personal concept of breathing or procession. Overall, the relations of the three are summarized in the concept of love, which involves a dynamic of both giving and receiving. The persons are what they are by virtue of what they give to and receive from each other. As such, they constitute the being of God, for there is no being of God underlying what the persons are to and from each other. God's being is a being in relation, without remainder relational.

But, and here we come to the second central concept, the fact that the relations are relations of love entails their freedom, which at least means their non-necessity. We have already met the claim that a trinitarian theology of creation involves the non-necessity of the world. The world does not have to be, because it is the outcome of the free creating act of the God who is already a relational being. But that is spoken of an action of God towards that which is not himself. What can it mean that the inner relations of the eternal God are free? Is not God always what he is, and therefore necessarily so? Bound up with that question is that of whether God's eternity entails a form of

---

[6] It is one of the merits of Hartshorne's analysis to show that the logic of an inadequately relational account of the God-world relation so easily collapses into pantheism: that there is not a very great distance from the causal definition of relation in the *Summa Theologiae* to the outright pantheism of Spinoza. Whether he can himself escape a form of pantheism is another matter. See especially Charles Hartshorne and W. L. Reese (eds.), *Philosophers Speak of God*, University of Chicago Press 1953.

necessity. Is it possible to speak of an eternal freedom?

One limit which is set for the discussion of this question is that in using concepts like relation and freedom of the being of God it must be emphasized that we are not attempting a map of the inner reality, only to say what we can of the God made known in Christ. In this case, it is being claimed that the freedom of the divine being is at the very least reflected in the freedom with which he enters into relation with that which is not himself. One conceptual link is to be found in the free obedience of Jesus, who is enabled by the Spirit to do the Father's will. If the incarnate Son's life is to be understood in terms of his free relation to the Father, it would seem to follow that there is in the divine eternity a freedom corresponding to it, so that to that freedom of God in creation and redemption, it can be argued – as Barth did argue at length – there corresponds what can only be called freedom in the relations of eternal Father, Son and Spirit.

The use of such an argument can be justified if it is held that freedom is a function of relations between persons and between persons and their world. Human freedom is what it is in a number of forms: in what takes place between God and man, man and man, and man and the world. What we thus have is an analogy of freedom, a freedom which takes a different shape in each case, appropriate to the character of the relation. What human freedom is can be understood only in the light of the freedom that is the gift of God through the Son and the Spirit. The question for this paper is whether the concept of the divine freedom from determination, revealed in God's freedom in creation, incarnation and redemption, is also of interest for the way we understand the structures of the non-personal created world.

That brings me to a third concept, one indicating the refusal of the early theologians to be content with a static doctrine of God. The concept of the divine energies appears to have developed as the result of thought about the divine activity in and towards the creation. Modern Orthodox theology, deriving from Palamas and what is probably excessive dependence on one letter of Basil, has tended to suggest an absolute distinction between the energies and the being of God. 'For Orthodox theology, the energies signify an exterior manifestation of the Trinity which cannot be interiorized, introduced, as it were, within the divine being, as its natural determination'.[7] But if 'Energies "proceed" from God and manifest His own being',[8] it is difficult to deny that just as the divine freedom expressed in the world derives from the inner freedom of God, here it must be so also. Otherwise, the being of God is essentially unknowable in an epistemologically destructive sense, leading possibly also to an entirely static and motionless concept of eternity along Aristotelian lines. If we are entitled to move to concepts of God's being consisting in free relatedness, may we not also argue that there is also a dynamic to God's being, corresponding to the dynamic of freedom and relatedness? It must be repeated that we are not here engaging in a mapping of the inner being of God, but asking what concepts we may develop in order to characterize the kind of being that God is. The doctrine of the Trinity, accordingly, is that theologoumenon developed, in response to Christian experience, to show that God's being is not motionless, impassible eternity but a personal *taxis* of dynamic and free relations.

IV. Historical Interlude

If the very being of God is dynamic and energetic, it is strange that Christian doctrines of creation should so often have taken static form. Of course, it never was denied that the creation involved movement and change, even though that change was not always welcomed as an essential part of the process. But the fact that eschatologies have often conceived the creation as simply returning to its starting point is a symptom of a kind of static conception. The same has happened with doctrines of salvation as effecting the restoration of human beings to a lost innocence, rather than as directing them to an eschatological goal, and these have at the same time had the effect of conceiving redemption not as something that happens in and with the rest of the created order, but as salvation from it. These things are said often enough, and scarcely need repeating now, except insofar as we need reminding that there is a considerable difference between neoplatonic and trinitarian conceptions of

---

[7] Vladimir Lossky, *The Mystical Theology of the Eastern Church*, London: James Clarke 1957, p. 80.

[8] Georges Florovsky, *Bible, Church and Tradition: An Eastern Orthodox View*, Belmont, Mass.: Nordland 1972, p. 117.

creation, and that the former often appear to have overridden the latter.

Indeed, what I want to suggest is that some modern scientific theories look as though they are the result of a process almost of intellectual evolution, from static theories owing more to Greek than to Christian influences to a dynamism reflecting the more eschatological emphasis of a doctrine that pays due attention to the role of the Holy Spirit. Here it is instructive to begin with a figure on the borderlands of modernity, who was also very much a theologian of the Holy Spirit, not least in his doctrine of creation, which to an extent shows the effect of its trinitarian dimension. 'For it is the Spirit who, everywhere diffused, sustains all things, causes them to grow, and quickens them in heaven and in earth.'[9]

Yet a recent study of Calvin as a sixteenth century figure shows that there is also a contradictory emphasis. William Bouwsma cites passages from the Reformer which indicate the influence of a pagan cosmology of a highly static kind. One quotation will make the point:

> Both Aristotle's unmoved mover and the spirituality of the heavenly bodies lurk behind Calvin's observation that 'God, when he revolves the world, remains consistent, so that what we call changes or turnings produce no variation in himself, but each revolution is coordinated with all the others.' He also slipped once into claiming that the heavens are 'eternal and exempt from alteration.'[10]

All this may be reason enough to see why Calvin opposed some of the claims of the new Copernican science. But even more modern figures retained very much a static view of things. Again, one quotation, this time from Prigogine and Stengers, whom we shall meet again later:

> In the classical view (sc. of the physical world) the basic processes of nature were considered to be deterministic and reversible. Processes involving randomness or irreversibility were considered only exceptions.[11]

---

[9] John Calvin, *Institutes of the Christian Religion*, I, xiii, 14.
[10] William J. Bouwsma, *John Calvin. A Sixteenth Century Portrait*, Oxford University Press 1988, p. 73.
[11] Ilya Prigogine and Isabelle Stengers, *Order Out of Chaos. Man's New Dialogue with Nature*, London: Fontana 1985, p. xxvii.

Determinism and reversibility both imply an essentially static universe, not in the sense that there is no movement, but that all that happens is decided in advance (determinism) and that any process can in theory be taken back the way it came. There is thus in principle no novelty. As in some forms of the ancient doctrine of creation, the end is not different from the beginning. The Newtonian cosmology thus shared some of the features of the essentially non-trinitarian doctrines of creation that tended to characterize the Western world before modern times.[12]

What has happened since Calvin's time is the development, partly under the impact of Christian theological impulses, of an increasingly dynamic conception of the universe. How far, or indeed whether at all, the the development should be attributed to specifically theological impulses is at present the subject of much debate, initiated in large part by Michael Foster's famous paper which claimed about half a century ago that certain aspects of the Christian doctrine of creation were necessary conditions for the development of modern science.[13] (In much of this he was anticipated by Pierre Duhem many years before.) The claim is now sometimes dogmatically asserted, sometimes, though not so often, questioned, as in the recent study by Funkenstein. Little certainty is likely to be obtained in historical judgements of this kind, though it must be significant that modern science happened in the Christian West and not somewhere else. 'Things happened thus and therefore, thus they must have happened.'[14]

My project here is the more modest one of showing some correspondences between ancient trinitarian and modern scientific conceptuality. If that happens to support Foster's contention, so much the better. But it is not historical claims in themselves that are theologically important. The heart of the matter is ontological. What kind of world do we live in, and what are we to do in and towards it? They are the central systematic and, indeed, existential and moral questions.

---

[12] It is remarkable how little Augustine's doctrine of creation is informed by trinitarian categories, in the sense that he does not articulate the doctrine christologically and pneumatologically.

[13] Michael B. Foster, 'The Christian Doctrine of Creation and the Rise of Modern Natural Science', *Mind* 43 (1934), pp. 446–68.

[14] R. Hooykaas, *Religion and the Rise of Modern Science*, Edinburgh: Scottish Academic Press 1972, p. 162.

V. Contingency, Relation and Energy

The three trinitarian concepts we have met are freedom, relation and energy. They are, as we have seen, interrelated in trinitarian theology, members of a cluster of linked concepts which attempt to characterize something of the being of God. I shall take them one at a time, inevitably involving overlap, and show how they, or something like them, appear in modern scientific conceptuality. Relation and energy are clearly concepts that appear in modern cosmology, and they will concern us eventually. But the joker in the pack is freedom. How does that fare when translated into the sphere of the physical world? The answer is that there can be no direct translation. Freedom is a word used of persons, divine and human, and can only in a highly questionable way be extended beyond that. Yet we have seen that the outcome of the free creation of the world by God is the otherness-in-relation of its being. It exists in its own way, but is none the less dependent for its existence on the activity of the creator. It is thus contingent upon God's creating, sustaining and redeeming action. Accordingly, it must be said that the concept of freedom is transmuted into contingence when we move from the personal to the non-personal sphere.

One meaning of contingence is of the world's dependence upon God for its being. But there is another meaning, and it is the one of which much has been made in recent writing. It means that the world does not *have* to be what or as it is. It is not the same as freedom, but is rather the way of speaking of the distinctive form of being of the non-personal created world. Persons have – or should have – freedom; that is a mark of their distinctive character, and, in the case of finite persons, of their being in the image of God. The strength of Process thought is that it recognizes the centrality of contingency; its weakness that it fails to distinguish between contingency and personality, so that everything has the same *kind* of freedom, albeit analogically. The claim here is that there is a qualitative – though not 'infinite qualitative' – distinction between freedom and contingency. Where persons have, or should have, freedom if they are to be themselves, the non-personal world is qualified by contingency.

As to that in which this contingency consists, there is,

inevitably, disagreement. It is as difficult to define as freedom, although it is worth observing that, according to Funkenstein, the modern notion appears to have its basis in scholastic disputes about the absolute and ordained power of God.[15] We shall therefore outline the claims of some recent essays in the subject, all of whose writers are agreed that, although the Newtonian conceptuality may hold for some levels of reality, as a means of accounting for the behaviour of the universe as a whole it has had its day. Like the First Evangelist, Arthur Peacocke states the difference between the old order and the new by means of a series of antitheses:

> Then . . . the natural world was regarded as mechanically determined and predictable . . . : *now* the world is regarded rather as the scene of the interplay of chance and of statistical, as well as causal, uniformity in which there is indeterminacy at the *micro*-level and unpredictability because of the complexity of causal chains at the *macro*-level, especially that of the biological.
> Then . . . the natural world was still regarded as static in form . . . essentially complete, unchanging and closed: *Now* it is discovered to be dynamic – a nexus of evolving forms, essentially incomplete . . . [16]

Like other similar theorists, Peacocke wishes to make it clear that indeterminacy does not imply the absence of causality. In fact it might be claimed that it is belief in the compossibility of the two that marks contemporary in contrast to classical science. According to Peacocke, the universe behaves in a law-like way, in which there operate networks of causally connected events. But the causality is not absolute – assimilated to some conception of logical necessity – for there is an '"openness" in the texture of the nexus of natural events which was not generally appreciated before the revolution in physics . . . in the first decade of this century'.[17]

In his *Divine and Contingent Order*, T. F. Torrance, whose general theological position is rather different from that of Peacocke, nevertheless develops a similar concept of contingency. His contribution is to link it specifically with the notion of

---

[15] Amos Funkenstein, *Theology and the Scientific Imagination from the Middle Ages to the Seventeenth Century*, Princeton University Press 1986, pp. 121ff.

[16] Arthur Peacocke, *Creation and the World of Science*, Oxford: Clarendon Press 1979, p. 62.

[17] Ibid., p. 59.

rationality. If once there was a tendency to identify the rational with the necessary, that is so no longer. The rationality of the world as discerned by modern science is located in patterns of things that are not bound to be what they are. It is a form of rationality, although it is essentially different from rationality as it is conceived by those philosophers who construe it on the model of logical necessity or euclidean geometry. 'Laws of nature . . . are not abstract generalizations, idealized laws prescinded from concrete, empirical reality, but objective contingent consistencies.'[18] That is to say, the rationality of scientific laws corresponds to the nature of the world, as non-necessary order: order that does not have to be as it is.

The notion of the contingence of the universe has been thrown into relief by recent accounts of the concept of chaos. This emphasizes even more strongly the idea of the world as contingent but ordered, and at the same time reveals something of the sheer mystery of that order. In his study of recent developments, the journalist James Gleick gives an account of those developments which show, as he claims, that the failure of long-range weather forecasting derived not from human incapacity to gather sufficient data on which to base a prediction, but from the impossibility of being able to make that kind of prediction. The world is such that inherent contingencies within its structure mean that minor alterations of initial conditions rule out the possibility of certain prediction. There is chaos but stability, that is to say, contingence but reliability. 'Chaos is ubiquitous; it is stable; it is structured.' It is, in fact, part of the dynamics of the universe. 'Those studying chaotic dynamics discovered that the disorderly behavior of simple systems acted as a *creative* process. It generated complexity: richly organised patterns, sometimes stable and sometimes unstable, sometimes finite and sometimes infinite, but always with the fascination of living things.'[19] The universe is not only contingent – free in its own way; but the contingency operates so as to be creative.

Gleick's book opens with what has become perhaps the pictorial symbol of the notion of chaos, the 'Butterfly Effect –

---

[18] T. F. Torrance, *Divine and Contingent Order*, Oxford University Press 1981, p. 38.
[19] James Gleick, *Chaos. Making a New Science*, London: Sphere Books 1987, pp. 76, 43.

the notion that a butterfly stirring the air today in Peking can transform storm systems next month in New York'.[20] The fact that this concrete example illustrates even more remarkable and mysterious phenomena – for example, that minute subatomic changes in gases on the other side of the universe can affect the way things happen on this side – leads us into the next phase of our discussion, of the character of the universe as a *perichoresis* of interrelated dynamic systems. We have already come across the notion, in the quotations from Peacocke, and it seems that here the development of modern field theory in Faraday and Clerk Maxwell – two of the predecessors to whom Einstein repeatedly refers – have led inexorably to the conceptual echo of trinitarian theology in relativity theory and its developments.

To obtain a measure of what has happened, and, indeed, to show how the change in cosmology is similar to, even caused by, a theological change, we must pause to glance at the history of the concept of relation. In Aristotle, and certainly in logic until the time of Kant, relation is subordinate to substance. Relations are what take place or subsist between substances that are prior to them: something first exists, and then enters or finds itself in relation to other things, which may change its accidents, but not what it really is (short of destroying it).[21] The notion is with us still, in the individualistic idea of a person as one who, in some measure already complete, enters into relations with other persons. Theologically speaking, Augustine deprived the concept of theological power by treating relation as ontologically intermediate between substance and accident, thus (1) identifying – or initiating the process which eventually identified – the person and the relation: the person, in God at any rate, *is* an eternal relation; and (2) rendering person subordinate to being in the reality of God. By reifying relations in that way, he made the concept effectively redundant.[22] The tragic side of the matter is to be found in Augustine's failure to appropriate the Cappadocian conceptual advance according to which relations are *between* persons – as the Aristotelian concept suggests – yet are at the same time *constitutive of* what those persons are – here against Aristotle. The persons are not

---

[20] Ibid., p. 8.

[21] Aristotle, *Categories*, ch. 7.

[22] For a detailed defence of this claim, see my *The Promise of Trinitarian Theology*, Edinburgh: T & T Clark 1991, ch. 3.

persons who then enter into relations, but are mutually constituted, made what they are, by virtue of their relations to one another.

What Augustine made effectively redundant in theology returns to transform science in the nineteenth and twentieth centuries. Relativity theory is the application of some such conception of relations as the trinitarian one just outlined to the universe. 'It (physics) now recognizes that, for an interaction to be real, the "nature" of the related things must derive from these relations, while at the same time the relations must derive from the "nature" of the things.'[23] Those words of Prigogine and Stengers lead us into the third of our concepts, that of energy, for it is evident that the physics of relativity also introduces a dynamism into the way things are conceived. There are no unchanging substances which enter into relations – as on the view of Aristotle and Newton alike – but the whole universe becomes conceivable as a dynamic structure of fields of force in mutually constitutive relations. To illustrate this dimension of the matter we turn to Prigogine's and Stengers' central claim in their study of cosmology. This is that the notion of evolution cannot be restricted to the organic sphere alone but must be applied to the universe as a whole. Their thesis illustrates something of the temporal irreversibility of the universe, its inherent directional dynamic.

Their repeated insistence is that science since Einstein has been forced to recognize what Einstein himself resisted, the inherent temporality of the cosmos. 'For us convinced physicists,' wrote Einstein, 'the distinction between past present and future is an illusion, though a persistent one.'[24] This means that Einstein's world, for all its relativity, remained finally static in the sense I have been using the word. Prigogine and Stengers are able to relate indeterminacy or contingence, relativity and a true dynamism. Theirs is a world whose reality is constituted by the arrow of time. It is a world congruent, though by no means identical, with that of Irenaeus, in the sense that it is consistent with his kind of eschatological dynamic.

There, of course, comes the difficulty. What is the relation between the kind of cosmological speculation in which these

---

[23] Prigogine and Stengers, *Order Out of Chaos*, p. 95.
[24] Ibid., p. 29f.

authors – or Capra[25] – engage, and a truly trinitarian eschatology? It is easy to generate, simply from the description of modern discoveries, a kind of secular or immanentist eschatology. But because trinitarian theology enables us to think of the world as at once absolutely other than God and completely dependent upon him, that step may be avoided. There is no absolute or necessary identity between the end of the universe as predicted by cosmologists and the eschatology that sees the end of the world as its perfection through the Holy Spirit. Nor, however, are we required to posit an absolute diastasis between the two. Trinitarian theology teaches that the world is destined for an absolute end, for perfection; it is directed to Christ, as it was created through him; but that through the action of the creator Spirit it is enabled to anticipate that end in the midst of time. We return to the concept of energies, and possibly to the Spirit as in some sense the energy of the Godhead. In such a way, we may understand the Holy Spirit as the divine energy releasing the energies of the world, enabling the world to realize its dynamic interrelatedness. Thus is God the Spirit conceived as the perfecting cause, the true source of the dynamic of the forward movement of the cosmos.

Yet, of course – and here we take leave of all optimistic, immanentist, progressive eschatologies: Peacocke, Process, Teilhard, and the rest – the dynamic of evolution is not coterminous with the dynamic of the Spirit, insofar as the latter is oriented to the one crucified in the midst of that very dynamic of energies of which we are speaking. That is to say, a theological account of creation must say that it has a destiny other than a continuing, if finite, progression to entropy and increasing complexity: the destiny of being enabled, through Jesus' offering of a perfect humanity to the Father, to praise its creator and return to him perfected. But there is overlap between the two, because the latter destiny is realized within the dynamics of the former. It is a far more complex matter than that revealed by scientific cosmology, because we shall have theologically to take account of such phenomena as evil and redemption. A merely natural theology of creation cannot take

[25] Fritjof Capra, *The Tao of Physics. An Exploration of the Parallels between Modern Physics and Eastern Mysticism*, London: Fontana 1983 (1st edition 1975).

full account of the place of evil and its overcoming, because it has no criteria other than those provided by the discoveries of the natural sciences.

Trinitarian theology may have assisted in the development of the concepts with the help of which modern science has made its discoveries of the relationality, contingence and dynamic of the universe, but a return must be made to theology proper if further questions than those merely immanent in science are to be asked: different kinds of questions, but not entirely independent, as some schools of science and theology have sometimes urged, but different within relation. What I am suggesting is a different way of conducting the dialogue between theology and the sciences: by means of a comparison and contrast of overlapping concepts. Where the same, or similar, concepts are used in theology and science – analogically, metaphorically, or whatever – there exists the possibility of conversation.

VI. Conclusion

What is the point of all this? The playing of conceptual games? Of this, two questions can be asked. The first is: How much hangs on the dialogue of science and religion which we all take with such earnestness? We return to one of the points of trinitarian theology as having somewhere near its centre the question about the nature of the world in which we live. A non-determined world is a place where human beings are called to be free, and that means to enter into free and personal relations with each other and relations of dialogue with the created universe. (Prigogine and Stengers' work is subtitled: *Man's New Dialogue with Nature*.) Very near the end of the book, those authors quote a few lines in which that splendid old sceptic Lucretius argues that in a determined universe, a universe without *clinamen*, there would be no room for human freedom.[26] The agreement with an Epicurean shows among other things that concepts of an undetermined universe are not the prerogative of Christian theologians, and that is why we must beware of claiming along with some modern theologians too much of the credit for the development of modern science. And in any case, the chief foes of Lucretius – determinism, superstition and the

---

26 Prigogine and Stengers, pp. 303–5.

anthropomorphic gods of the ancient world – are also ours. There we find the heart of the matter, that we are here engaged not merely in a dialogue between science and theology, but in an encounter between what makes for life and what for death. Ontology and ethics, creation and redemption, cannot be treated apart from one another.

The second question takes us to matters of similarly redemptive import. Suppose that we are able to transcend some of the weaknesses of the traditions of Plato and Kant, and to find a way of suggesting, even in the light of modern historical understanding, a way in which words and the world in some way have a purchase on one another. What is the gain? We have already seen that we find concepts with the help of which we are enabled to come to terms with the being of God, ourselves and the created world. But, more important, we can also begin to find a way out of the cultural fragmentation that so bedevils the modern world. George Steiner has argued that in 'the break of the covenant between word and world' there has taken place 'one of the very few revolutions of spirit in Western history'.[27] Against that breach of covenant, the thrust of this paper is to suggest that the history of words, even words of metaphysical import, is not a field on which empty battles have been fought, nor is it one in which no progress is made in understanding the way things are. One of the things that the sciences have to teach – despite the relativistic scepticism of some modern philosophers of science – is that through the disciplined use of the imagination real insight in the meaning of things can be found and expressed in words.

The important lesson for the modern world to learn is that this is of far more than merely scientific import. If the fragmentation and relativism that are the message of some writers in the humanities are to have the last word, the outlook for human community and human action in the world is bleak. With the loss of a common language there is lost also that communication without which we are unable to live together and in the world. The renewal of language is thus the precondition for the renewal of social order. Such renewals will come when due attention is given to the doctrine of creation, not in

---

[27] George Steiner, *Real Presences. Is there anything in what we say?* London: Faber & Faber 1989, p. 93.

abstraction from the doctrine of redemption, but as its counterpart. If the latter is neglected, the sin and evil that prevent the creation from becoming what it is called to be are ignored, and thus allowed to run their course unhindered. That is the danger of the sentimentalizing of creation to be found in much creation spirituality. But any treatment of redemption apart from its context, the creation, divorces human being from the world of which it is apart and to whose care it has been entrusted.

And so we return to the doctrine of the Trinity. As we have seen, the doctrine enables us to understand the world as truly itself, because created real and good by God, but also what it is only in continued dependence upon his conserving action. Creation through the Son and the Spirit ensures the affirmation both of the relatedness of the world to its maker and its dynamic teleology, its directedness to eschatological perfection. But it should never be forgotten that the doctrine is one forged under the impact of redemption, and specifically of that brought about by the incarnation, death, resurrection and ascension, achieved by through the work of the eschatological Spirit, of the one through whom the world was made. Its function is thus to hold in relation the two central concerns of theological thought, creation and redemption, while distinguishing them.

A truly trinitarian doctrine of creation is a prime desideratum for modern Christian theology because only by its means can the basis be laid for a proper alternative to the platonic and Kantian options, with an account of whose strengths and weaknesses this paper began. Through it we shall learn to think, after both of those seminal thinkers, of the world as open to human language and the discovery of meaning, and yet, both because of its thralldom to evil and because of the mysterious depths given it by its creator, also beyond the kind of final philosophical grasp that both of those thinkers in their different ways sought. World and word are thus to be understood as open to each other, but as so only through a process involving the redemption of human capacity and in a way that eludes any final conceptualization that would in effect cancel the openness. Our words can grasp only at anticipations of final truth, but they are through grace anticipations none the less. In such a case, the historicity of language is not a threat to the possibility of its expressing truth, but a positive gain, for history is the means by which the world is redeemed and brought to its proper perfection in Christ.

6. Christology and Trinitarian Thought

Christoph Schwöbel

I. Crisis in Christology

It is not a sign of great originality to observe that modern Christology is in a state of crisis. There is nothing new about this situation, nor about the observation. Indeed, it could be said that this crisis has accompanied modern Christology since its inception, so that the term 'modern Christology' and the description 'Christology in crisis' are almost equivalents. The ills which plague present-day Christology have been with it for the last 250 years and their effects are today no less painful than they were when they were first felt in the days of Reimarus and Lessing. This is not least documented by the fact that the past two centuries have been times of intense christological reflection, carried out by a variety of theological schools and individual theologians in all denominations of Western Christianity. The frequency with which a 'christocentric' approach to the whole enterprise of Christian theology has been demanded is in every case a sign for the seriousness of the situation, even if it does not in all cases offer indications that it is being overcome. It is perhaps not an exaggeration to say that Christian theology has – for better or worse – learnt to live with the crisis, and that to a large extent christological reflection has, more or less openly, assumed the character of crisis-management where the deeper causes of the crisis are ignored in order to contain its most threatening immediate effects.

By calling this situation a situation of crisis I want to express the urgency of the modern challenge to Christology. It may therefore be helpful to recall the constitutive elements of a crisis in order to see what is at stake in this situation.[1] Phenomeno-

---

[1] The following description of what constitutes a crisis owes much to Wilfried Härle, 'Krise in theologischer Sicht', *Wege zum Menschen* 28

logically a crisis can be seen as comprising the following characteristics:

– it constitutes a threat to the being of an individual or a community which can concern its very existence, the validity of its meaning system and its identity;

– it is necessarily ambivalent, its outcome is still open;

– it does not come unprepared, but is the culmination of often hidden factors and forces which have been there for a long time, but whose threatening potential is suddenly actualized;

– it is a disruption of the 'normal' course of events;

– it divides the past and the future so that the appropriation of the past in the present determines the possibilities of the future; and:

– last but not least, it necessitates change.

When we apply this phenomenology of a crisis situation to the state of modern Christology, we can see that the christological crisis indeed goes very deep: the continued existence of Christianity and the identity of Christian theology depend on how Christians understand the identity of Jesus Christ. Therefore the crisis in Christology cannot be brushed aside as something that is of minor significance. If this situation is a crisis, it is still an open question whether it can be resolved. Successful crisis-management can delay the outcome, but cannot decide it. If the situation of Christology in modern times fits the description of a crisis, then the elements which constituted the challenge of the Enlightenment to Christology can be expected to have a pre-history in earlier Christian thought, they cannot simply be ascribed to a sudden alien invasion of Christian theology from the outside. Furthermore, so long as the christological crisis is not resolved, the attempt to go on doing 'business as usual' in Christian theology and in the Christian churches may prove to be an exercise in self-deception. If seeing the situation of modern Christology as a crisis is an apt description, it is unrealistic to hope that the ills of modern Christology can be healed by a simple repristination of traditional 'orthodoxy'. The past that has to be appropriated will always be one that has offered inadequate resources for preventing or combating the modern crisis of christological thought. Only if these inadequacies are appropriated as well and can be remedied, can one hope to point

(1977), pp. 408–16.

to future possibilities of overcoming the christological crisis. The changes which are necessitated by this crisis can therefore neither consist in attempts at turning the clock of theological history back to less critical times, nor can they hope to offer a solution to the crisis that leaves the classical paradigms of christological reflection completely behind. The changes which can be initiated as first and, no doubt, modest steps of resolving the crisis and not as symptoms of its continuing virulence will have to overcome the alternative between theological traditionalism and modernism.

What are, then, the ills that have haunted modern Christology for most of its history, and what are the symptoms which characterize its persistent state of crisis? Perhaps it is possible to summarize the critical assumptions in three groups. First of all, there is the antinomy between what can be called 'the historical' and 'the ultimate', expressed with brilliant clarity in Lessing's thesis that contingent truths of history can never become the proof of necessary truths of reason.[2] This contrast can be expressed in a variety of forms, all of which have, at one time or another, formed part of the background of Christology's modern history. It can be construed as the antinomy between contingent being and necessary being, as the contrast between the temporal and the eternal and as the divide that separates history from the realm of metaphysical ultimates. It has frequently been pointed out that these contrasts in their varied forms of expression represent one of the most influential and formative elements of the heritage of Platonism in Western thought.[3] This heritage consists not so much in the specific way in which the eternal being of forms was contrasted to the transitory existence of the world of appearance in Platonism, but in the habit, deeply ingrained in Western thought, of conceiving the relationship between the contingent, historical, empirical and temporal and the necessary, metaphysical, rational and eternal as one of logical and ontological opposition. It is perhaps due to the incomplete Christianization of Hellenism[4] that the philo-

---

[2] Cf. G. E. Lessing, *Über den Beweis des Geistes und der Kraft* (1777), in *Lessing's Theological Writings: Selections in Translation*, Eng. trans. Henry Chadwick, A. & C. Black 1956, p. 53.

[3] Cf. Colin E. Gunton, *Yesterday and Today. A Study of Continuities in Christology*, London: Darton, Longman & Todd 1983, esp. pp. 86–102.

[4] I Take this expression from R. W. Jenson, 'Second Locus: The Triune God', in Carl E. Braaten and Robert W. Jenson (eds.), *Christian Dogmatics*,

sophical theology of Christianity has sometimes more contributed to this dualism than to its overcoming.

In Christology the problem is, of course, particularly clear in
the two-natures doctrine when the divine nature and human
nature are construed in terms of the logical complements of the
kind–essences of divinity and humanity. As long as christological reflection is conducted within the framework of the
Chalcedonian definition this constituted a major problem for
christological reflection, but it could be contained by the
assertion of the unity of the person of Christ and theologians
were therefore obliged to give an account of Christ without
confusion or separation of the contrasted natures. But as soon as
the investigation of the problems of Christology was no longer
conducted within that framework the underlying dualistic
tendencies reasserted themselves with undiminished force. This
resulted in the combination of a philosophical theism with a
more or less historical Jesuology in many conceptions of the
Enlightenment.[5] The separation between a historical account of
the person of Jesus and a theological account of the ultimate
reality of God and Christ is now a regular feature in the problematical relationship between much of biblical studies and
dogmatic theology where one is conceived as a historical discipline and the other concerned with the reflection of ahis-
torical ultimates, and where both have developed their 'noli-
me-tangere'-attitude into respectable methodological principles. In systematic theology this antinomy is today most
frequently presented as a central problem of method: should it
proceed from above or from below, from the historical reality of
the person of Jesus of Nazareth or from the ultimate being of
God.[6]

Philadelphia: Fortress Press 1984, pp. 118ff: 'The Initial Christianizing of
Hellenism'.

[5] The outstanding representative of this view is, of course, Hermann
Samuel Reimarus, cf. *Reimarus: Fragments,* Eng. trans. Ralph S. Fraser,
London: SCM Press 1971. I have argued in another context that the
disjunction of the doctrine of God and the doctrine of Christ has a
programmatic function in the project of philosophical theism in the
eighteenth century; cf. my essay 'After Post-Theism', in: Svend Anderson
(ed.), *Theism: Tradition and Modernity,* Aarhus: Aarhus University Press
1994, pp. 157–91, esp. pp. 168–76.

[6] Cf. Nicholas Lash, 'Up and Down in Christology', in S. Sykes and D.
Holmes (eds.), *New Studies in Theology,* London: Duckworth 1980, pp. 31–
46.

Secondly, there is the antinomy between the past and the present, also memorably expressed in Lessing's metaphor of the 'ugly broad ditch' that separates us from the past.[7] How is it possible that an event in the past has ultimate significance in the present? And how is it conceivable that past events which we know from the testimony of witnesses almost two millennia ago should determine our present certainties about the fundamental structures of our understanding of reality? These questions received a particular urgency with the rise of historical consciousness which suddenly created a distance between the biblical narrative and its contents and present-day readers and hearers. This distance disrupted the universe of meaning, shaped by the biblical narrative, which comprehended for the Fathers as well as for the Reformers Adam, Christ and their own life in the horizon of God's mighty acts.[8] In our own times Lessing's ditch has been widened into an abyss which according to the theories of historical relativism not only separates our time from that of the events of the biblical tradition, but also implies an unbridgeable gulf between the language, the knowledge and even the reality of Christianity's foundational document, the conciliar decisions of the first five centuries and our present attitudes and beliefs.

It is against this background that for Christology the quest for the historical Jesus and the question 'Who is Jesus Christ for us today?' can be seen as alternatives. What seems no longer possible in modern Christology is to present an integrated picture of Jesus Christ's past and his presence for the church and the cosmos. The critical effects of this antinomy between past and present are most clearly apparent in the difficulty of describing the christological presuppositions of the eucharist which is in any case – as the debates between the different strands of Reformation theology show – the ultimate testing-ground for the validity of a christological conception. And again, it is in the area of questions concerning the method of Christology that this antinomy is most acutely felt: in the question of whether the approach to Christology should proceed from the historical Jesus or from the *Christus praesens* of contemporary Christian experience of faith.[9]

---

[7] *Lessing's Theological Writings*, p. 55.
[8] Cf. Hans W. Frei, *The Eclipse of Biblical Narrative. A Study in Eighteenth and Nineteenth Century Hermeneutics*, New Haven and London: Yale University Press 1974, pp. 1–50.

The third antinomy which makes a significant contribution to the modern crisis in Christology is the disjunction of being and meaning. The tendency which I want to refer to may already be present in Melanchthon's famous dictum that to know Christ is to know his benefits for us and not to contemplate, like the schoolmen, his natures and the modes of the Incarnation (*Christum cognoscere est beneficia eius cognoscere, non, quod isti [sc. scholastici theologistae] eius naturas, modos incarnationis contueri*)[10] – in 1521 perhaps a justified protest against the mushrooming of theoretical speculation in Christology in later medieval thought. It then becomes a dominant theme in the christological conceptions of Albrecht Ritschl and his school. For contemporary Christology it received its most influential form in Rudolf Bultmann's christological reflections where it is combined with our first two antinomies. Since historical investigation cannot give a foundation for faith in Christ and since faith in Christ depends on the call to decision which confronts us in the *kerygma* in the present, the christological issue is not what we can say about the being of Christ (which in any case would present us with an objectifying image of Christ), but what we can assert about his significance, and that means his meaning for the possibility of being granted authenticity in our existence today. The contrast between meaning and being is in this way understood as an expression of the relationship of the work and the person of Christ, and it is claimed that the work of Christ, soteriology, is the only legitimate access to Christology whereas metaphysical reflection on his being, his person can only lead us to inadequate notions of God and salvation.[11]

It is equally symptomatic for this antinomy that Wolfhart Pannenberg in his, to a large extent fully justified, critique of this

---

[9] The approach to Christology from the present experience of Christ in the Christian community is a characteristic feature of the so-called 'Erlangen school' of Lutheran theologians in the nineteenth century, cf. Franz Hermann Reinhold Frank, *System der christlichen Gewißheit*, vol. I, Erlangen 1870, pp. 303ff.

[10] *Loci communes* of 1521, CR 21, 85; *Melanchthons Werke in Auswahl*, ed. Robert Stupperich, Gütersloh: Gütersloher Verlagshaus, vol. II, 1 (1952), p. 7.

[11] This is boldly put by Paul Tillich: 'Christology is a function of soteriology. The problem of soteriology creates the christological question and gives direction to the christological answer.' *Systematic Theology*, vol. II, Chicago: University of Chicago Press 1957, p. 174.

approach in *Jesus – God and Man* argues that Christology has to start from the person of Jesus Christ, but immediately equates this approach with the approach from below, from the Jesus of history.[12] From this starting-point one can only develop an understanding of the being of the person of Christ as the last stage of a complicated argument from his history to the retroactive ontological implications of the resurrection. The antinomy which is one of the crisis-symptoms of modern Christology seems to confront us with the choice between a non-soteriological ontology (being without meaning) and a non-ontological soteriology (meaning without being). With regard to this question we are again referred to the area of questions of method as it becomes apparent in the different approaches of Bultmann and Pannenberg: should christological reflection proceed from Christology to soteriology or from soteriology to Christology?

The fact that all three antinomies which are constitutive for the modern crisis of Christology have their clearest expression in problems of method is itself a crisis-symptom. In view of the modern challenges to Christology the substantive problems of Christology present themselves as problems of method in a very fundamental sense: they are seen to be decisive for the success or failure of establishing new foundations for the problematical enterprise of doing Christology.

When we attempt to summarize the state of crisis of modern Christology from its symptoms, we have to conclude that we are presented with a picture of disintegration.[13] Modern Christology seems to be increasingly unable to conceive and to conceptualize the unity of the person of Christ and seems to be left with the fragments of the 'historical Jesus', the 'Christ of faith' and the 'Son of God' of christological Dogma. Therefore modern Christological reflection seems mainly concerned with finding ways of integrating the fragments in a new synthesis, of joining together what has been put asunder.

---

[12] W. Pannenberg, *Grundzüge der Christologie*, Gütersloh: Gütersloher Verlagshaus 1964, p. 42: 'Die Soteriologie muß aus der Christologie folgen, nicht umgekehrt. Sonst verliert gerade der Heilsglaube selbst jede Grundlage ... die Christologie muß ausgehen von dem damaligen Jesus, nicht von seiner Bedeutsamkeit für uns'.

[13] For a similar description of the symptoms of the ills of modern Christology, though different suggestions for their diagnosis and therapy cf. Robert Morgan, 'Non Angli sed Angeli: Some Anglican Reactions to German Gospel Criticism', in S. Sykes and D. Holmes (eds.), *New Studies in Theology*, pp. 1–30.

II. Christology and the Trinitarian Logic
of Christian Discourse about God

The crisis of modern Christology which we have described with
regard to some of its main groups of symptoms is a complex phenomenon, and any attempt at diagnosing the character of the ills
of modern Christology in order to consider a prescription for their
therapy must attempt to do justice to this complexity. It appears,
however, that many of the complex aspects of the crisis of modern Christology which point to equally complex causes, are
connected so that they form aspects of a common syndrome. We
are therefore not dealing with a simple and unified phenomenon
which could be subject to a monocausal explanation and diagnosis, but with a syndrome in which many aspects come together
which nevertheless seem to be closely related. My proposal for
the diagnosis can be expressed in the thesis: The crisis in modern
Christology is due to the neglect of the trinitarian logic of the
Christian understanding of God and its implications for the
Christian understanding of what it means to be human. It is
because of the trinitarian 'forgetfulness' of much of modern
Western theology that Christology gets entangled in the antinomies of the historical and the ultimate, past and present,
meaning and being which constitute important aspects of the
crisis of modern Christology. Initially, this diagnosis can be
supported by two connected observations. Wherever the understanding of God in modern theology is characterized by a radical
rejection of the trinitarian character of the Christian understanding of God, the problems of Christology become intractable
to the point where the whole enterprise of doing Christology is
abandoned. And conversely, where there is a strong awareness of
the trinitarian character of Christian faith in God new possibilities are opened up for resolving the antinomies in which
modern Christology seems to be trapped, and this applies – for
all one might want to criticize in their conceptions – to Hegel as
well as to Barth and to Wolfhart Pannenberg's new *Systematic
Theology*.

Furthermore, it seems that many modern debates about
Christology are at best conducted in a binitarian framework
sometimes supplemented by an impersonal understanding of the

Spirit. If this is seen as the fundamental form of the issues, it can happen that both parties in the debate, those urging for a modernist replacement of Christology and those defending the traditional Christology of conciliar orthodoxy remain trapped in the antinomies of the modern crisis of Christology – a state of affairs which in my view is evidenced by the debate about *The Myth of God Incarnate*. Heroic appeals for a return to Chalcedon can therefore be just as much symptoms of the crisis as programmatic pleas to abandon the christological quest. The fact that the clarification of trinitarian logic of the Christian understanding of God preceded the attempt at defining the boundaries of orthodox Christology should be seen as an important hint that elucidation of the doctrine of Christ necessarily presupposes the trinitarian understanding of God as its basis.

In attempting to sketch the trinitarian logic of Christian faith I can only point to a number of vital features and in doing so rely on the seminal work of others in this area. It is doubtful whether Christian theology would ever have developed a doctrine of the Trinity, if it had not retained the Hebrew Scriptures as the necessary framework for the experience, identification, predication of God in Christian faith. Robert Jenson therefore refers to the Hebrew Scriptures as 'the Root of Trinitarianism'.[14] I can here concentrate on a number of crucial elements. Israel identified her God according to the one dominant strand which underlies many of the theological traditions of the Hebrew Scriptures by the proper name 'Jahweh' and by identifying descriptions which referred to Jahweh as the author of particular historical acts in time for the salvation of his people. This identification of God is interpreted as grounded in his self-identification to Israel as her God in specific disclosure-experiences in the temporal sequence of history. This self-identification of Jahweh as Israel's God in addressing his people and in his action in history is paradigmatically summarized in the introductory formula to the Ten Commandments: 'I am Jahweh, your God, who brought you out of the land of Egypt' (Ex. 20:3). Reference to the Exodus as the paradigm of God's self-identifying action structures Israel's experience: It is in looking back on this event in the past that Israel is enabled to under-

---

[14] R. W. Jenson, 'The Triune God', pp. 102–5.

stand its present as qualified by Jahweh's action as judgement and mercy in the future. The narrative identification of Jahweh as the only way to depict his self-identification by name and identifying description cannot be transcended into a straight-forward metaphysical description of the being of God. Con-sequently, it is in the narratively identified and described character of Jahweh that Israel's future rests and which is its only warrant.

There is, however, a second dominant strand in the way in which Israel talked about her God, represented predominantly but not exclusively in the traditions of Wisdom literature, which shows many similarities to aspects of the thought of her ancient Near Eastern neighbours. Here God is understood as the sustainer and guarantor of the world-order which owes its being, its ordered structures and its meaning to God's righteousness. God is the one who upholds the cosmic, moral and social order of the world so that everything that happens is dependent on him and so that human beings can in their deeds correspond to the order established by God's wisdom.[15]

This belief in the world-order of God's righteousness, estab-lished by Wisdom and apprehended in wisdom, is not left as it is, but in many important strands of the theological and literary traditions of the Hebrew Scriptures it is modified through its interaction with the narrative identification of God in the particularity of events in the temporal sequence of history. The astonishing claim that underlies this development is that the God who is identified by the name Jahweh and by the identi-fying descriptions referring to his mighty acts is indeed the creative ground of all being, meaning and salvation in the world. Therefore a conception of creation could be developed which understands the creation as a dynamic process with a beginning in time which is continued in a story of covenants, Exodus and exile. The interaction between both strands is further docu-mented by the fact that the Exodus can be described in the lan-guage of creation as the imposition of order over the forces of chaos. This identification of the God of the Exodus and of God as the power of righteousness is behind the prophetic criticism

---

[15] Cf. for a summary account: Ulrich Luck, 'Weisheitsüberlieferungen vom Alten zum Neuen Testament', in Hans-Joachim Klimkeit (ed.), *Biblische und außerbiblische Spruchweisheit*, Studies in Oriental Religions vol. 20, Wiesbaden: Otto Harrasowitz 1991, pp. 7–31.

which is directed both at Israel's forgetfulness of the promise of the God of the Exodus and its violation of God's rule of right-eousness. For this reason faith could hold fast to the belief that God's righteousness will be ultimately victorious even where this trust seemed to be falsified by present experience, because the God of righteousness was seen as the God who identified himself as the God of the Exodus and the God who promises the liberation of his covenant people.

The attempt at combining the understanding of the partic-ularity of the God who identifies himself in the temporal acts of history and the universality of the God who will establish his righteousness in the world lies at the roots of Israel's eschato-logical hopes, from messianic expectations, to the nations' pilgrimage to Zion and to the apocalyptic visions of the ulti-mate revelation of God's righteousness. What is of utmost importance for the understanding of God in the New Testament is that the identification of God in both strands which appear in the Hebrew Scriptures in many forms and combinations is retained and transformed by its application to the experience of Christ. The name of Jesus becomes an accepted way of addressing and invoking the God of Israel so that this name is employed to refer to the self-identification of the God of Israel in Jesus – a fact that is reflected, almost exclusively in modern theology, in Karl Barth's use of the name of Jesus to designate the task and content of Christology.[16] New identifying descriptions for the God of Israel are introduced in which the story and destiny of Jesus becomes the focus for God's self-identification. These identifying descriptions, exemplified perhaps most clearly in expressions like 'the God who raised Jesus our Lord from the dead' (Rom. 4:25), show very clearly the claim that is made in the New Testament. For the first Christians it is no longer possible to identify the God of Israel apart from reference to Jesus, and it is not possible to describe the identity of Jesus apart from reference to the God of Israel. The conjunction of the identification of God and the identification of Jesus implies that

---

[16] For Barth it is only the 'name Jesus Christ' which expresses both the movement of God to humanity and the exaltation of humanity to God: 'Eine Beides zugleich und in Einem erfassende Aussage ist im Neuen Testament eigentlich nur der Name Jesus Christus, der wie die Trennung des Einen vom Anderen so auch ihre Aufhebung in einem beide verschmelzenden Dritten verbietet und unmöglich macht.' *Kirchliche Dogmatik* IV/1, p. 149. Earlier in this work he can even say: 'Dieser Name ist Gottes Offenbarung.' (KD I/2, p. 11f.)

the christological title-terms which are predicated of Jesus are as much statements about the being and action of the God of Israel as about Jesus. This also explains why Jesus' addressing God as the Father and the church's invocation of Jesus as the Son could become the paradigm for the use of all other christological models, since the Father-Son relationship exemplifies the mutuality and reciprocity of God's self-identification in Jesus and the identification of Jesus through his relation to God. The self-identification of God in Christ exemplifies the same particularity and temporal structure as the self-identification of God in the events of Israel's history. It therefore has an irreducible narrative form.

At the same time we find in the New Testament also that the second strand of Israel's talk about Jahweh is taken up and transformed by the experience of Christ. Christ is included in the view of God as the unconditional ground of all being, meaning and righteousness. He is described as the one in whom everything is created (Col. 1:16) as the Logos who was with God through whom all things came to be (Joh. 1:1ff.) and in whom God's righteousness is made victorious. The truly astonishing assertion of Christian faith as it finds expression in the New Testament in a way which starkly reflects the scandal of the Gospel, is that in Jesus the righteousness of God is realized in the finality and unconditionality which constitutes its universality for all who accept it in faith as their justification. This is at the core of the message of the resurrection of the one who was crucified. The claim made in these statements means nothing less than that the righteousness of God the creator, the eschatological truth of all meaning and being, is victorious in the temporal life, death and resurrection of Christ as the reconciliation of God with the alienated creation. However, if the reconciliation of God with creation is truly unconditional, dependent on nothing but God's being of love, then the relationship between Father and Son which constitutes Christ as the agent of salvation cannot be a temporal and transitory accident of God's being, but has to be seen as eternally rooted in God's being.

What may not be forgotten is that these identifications of God in Christ which are, already in the New Testament and increasingly so in the second century, expressed in his identification as the Son of the Father are formulated from the post-

Pentecost perspective of the absence of Christ in the flesh and of the experience of the presence of the God who is disclosed in Christ, the God who is the Father and Son, in the Spirit. The traditional ways of talking about the Spirit of God in the Hebrew Scriptures, the creative power of God in action who enables creation to respond in its life to the will of the creator and the power of God's future at work in the here and now, is now carefully qualified so that talking of the Spirit becomes a way of identifying God again in the situation of the absence of the earthly Jesus. The Spirit is therefore understood as the Spirit of Christ insofar as the Spirit makes the reality of God's right-eousness as it is realized in Jesus present for those who confess Jesus as the Lord and in this way makes the believers co-present with Christ and thus enables them to participate by grace as God's daughters and sons in the relationship of the Son to the Father. The Spirit is also conceived as the Spirit of God insofar as the Spirit who leads believers through the Son to the Father is the Spirit who from the beginning energizes God's creation by bringing it to its eschatological fulfilment.

If the Spirit who as the presence of God in the absence of the earthly Jesus is the Spirit who is from the beginning the giver of life to God's creation and the power of God's eschatological fulfilment, then the Spirit cannot only be understood as being *consequent upon* the Christ-event as the Spirit of truth, but must also be seen as being *constitutive for* the Christ-event. Just as the Spirit re-presents the relationship of Father and Son in the absence of Jesus in the flesh, so he is also constitutive for this relationship as it is enacted from Jesus' birth over his baptism through his life and death to his resurrection. The structure which appears in this conception can be expressed in the follow-ing way: The Spirit through whom the Father relates to the Son and the Son to the Father is the Spirit through whom the Father relates through the Son to the church, and through whom the church relates through the Son to the Father. Ironically, it is one of the side-effects of the concentration of orthodox Christology on the doctrine of the two natures in Western theology that it has obscured the way in which significant strands of the theological traditions of the New Testament see the Spirit as much as constitutive for the Christ-event as they describe the presence of the Spirit for the believers as a consequence of the Christ-event.

What can be called the *trinitarian logic of Christian faith* takes shape in the New Testament in a number of related developments and is expressed in a pluriform variety of different modes of expression, metaphors, models and paradigms. Identifying descriptions are presented which identify God with reference to the message, life, cross and resurrection of Jesus and are related to identifying descriptions of Jesus which determine Jesus' identity by reference to the God of Israel. The present experience of the Christian community of salvation in God is ascribed to the agency of the Spirit who is identified as the Spirit of God and the Spirit of Christ. In the varied combinations of these identity descriptions the temporal structure of God's self-identification is not transcended into the eternal Now of the divine presence, nor is it simply reduced to successive stages of divine manifestation. God's self-identification in Christ is not seen as simply superseding the God of Israel, nor is the contingent re-presentation of Christ to the believers in the Spirit understood as the *Aufhebung,* the sublation, of God's self-identification in the history and destiny of Jesus. The temporal particularity of God's self-identification is retained in the way in which the three identifying descriptions are related. The Spirit does not present another God than the story of Jesus and Jesus points away from himself to the one he calls Father. The believers who are brought into the fellowship of the Holy Spirit are by the grace of Christ included in his relationship of sonship to the Father. The eschatological movement of God's love brackets the temporal identification of God in Israel, in Jesus and in the Spirit. And this can be developed in both ways: in the way in which the Spirit refers to Jesus and to God the Father and in the way in which the action of God the Father in the Son is perfected in the Spirit.

It is, however, important to note that the temporal identification of God as Father, Son and Spirit which is bracketed in the eschatological ultimacy of God's action for the salvation of creation is, from very early on, combined with the identification of God as the unconditional ground of being, meaning and righteousness. Message, life, cross and resurrection of Jesus Christ are the ultimate and unconditional victory of God's righteousness. The reconciliation of the creator with his creation is seen as the consummation of the relationship God intended for the creation from the beginning. The eschatological ultimacy of what happens at Easter and Pentecost makes it impossible to see Jesus and the Spirit as merely transitory stages of the realization of God's will, but requires to see them as permanently belonging to God's being. Because the Son and the Spirit are not external to God's being, the Son and the Spirit can be seen as active in all divine works from creation to the consummation in the Kingdom. The eschatological ultimacy of the temporal identification of the Father, the Son and the Spirit requires a recognition of their ontological ultimacy for the being of God. When the early Christian communities invoked God the Father, the Son and the Spirit, baptized in the triune name and addressed God the Father, through the Son in the Spirit, they did not merely recall past manifestations of God, nor did they refer to transitory appearances of an immutable divine essence, nor did they spiritually climb a ladder with increasing degrees of transcendence. They were relating to a God who could only be addressed and who could only be proclaimed in the framework of this trinitarian structure.

I am, of course, not claiming that we can offer scriptural proof for a developed doctrine of the Trinity in the New Testament. I would, however, claim that we detect in the expressions of Christian practice in worship, proclamation, reflection and action an underlying *proto-trinitarian depth structure* which provides the focus for the identity of the Christian message and defines the framework for the pluriformity of the rich variety of expressions of Christian faith. It also set the agenda for the further development of Christian theology, in which the explication of this trinitarian faith and the elucidation of the experience of reality from this perspective interacted with the identity-definition of Christian faith with regard to those on the fringes of the Christian communities and with the proclamation and apologetic defence of this faith to those outside. The process which is, following Harnack, commonly described as the Hellenization of Christianity owes at least as much and probably more to the need for clarification and the positive possibilities for explication implied in this proto-trinitarian structure of faith than to the assimilation and adaptation to Hellenistic thought-forms and should therefore more properly be seen as the *interaction* between the Hellenization of Christianity and the Christianization of Hellenism. Both processes remained incomplete and form part of the ambivalent heritage of patristic thought to modern theology.

It is this trinitarian logic of Christian faith which provided the framework in which christological reflection on the identity of Jesus Christ developed. It is one of the main features of this trinitarian framework that it allowed the retention and co-existence of the rich variety of christological predications, models and paradigms and of christological narratives and hymns in the New Testament and in the early church. It also provided the vital criteria for the processes of construction and criticism in christological thought in the first centuries. Christologies claiming to offer a unitary framework for discourse about Jesus which denied the reality of the particular, material and temporal self-identification of God in Jesus were rejected (as, for example, the various forms of Docetism), just as christologies which although they emphasized the temporal structure and historical reality of Jesus's story denied that he is in an un-conditional and ultimate sense part of God's being (and not only in a conditional and derivative sense as the various versions of Ebionitism or Adoptianism suggested). The point is, however, not that one group of heresies correctly stated the divinity of Christ, but neglected the humanity whereas the other group's mistake is the converse of this mistake. From the perspective of the trini-tarian logic of Christian faith it has to be said that the divinity of Christ cannot be correctly grasped where his temporal and material humanity is denied, and that his humanity cannot be properly understood even in its temporal structure and historical reality, if it is not seen as the self-identification of God in the reality of a human life. The solution to the christological prob-lem is not a compromise between the Docetist understanding of the divinity of Christ and the Ebionite understanding of his humanity. This may be one factor why the trinitarian logic of Christian faith had to find a more satisfactory concept-ualization, before the christological debate could progress with any promise of theological advance.

III. The Doctrine of the Trinity and Christology

It is impossible to go here through all the different stages and strands which contributed to a coherent conceptualization of the trinitarian logic of Christian faith in the theology of the

Cappadocians and its conciliar affirmation at Constantinople. We can, however, retrace a few of the steps in the development that prepared the ground for the theological creativity of the Cappadocians. This will give us an indication of the implications of the trinitarian logic of Christian faith. For the sake of brevity a brief summary may suffice:

1. There is Irenaeus' response to the challenge presented by the different groups of Gnosticism which offered a christocentric conception of salvation, but introduced a radical division into the understanding of God, by separating the imperfect God of the evil material creation from the God of salvation understood as complete liberation from the materiality of created existence. To counter this tendency Irenaeus employed the trinitarian logic of faith in order to assert the unity of the divine economy: the God of creation is the God of salvation and of the final consummation, and this God is the Father working through his 'two hands' the Son and the Spirit.[17] This trinitarian emphasis on the unity of the divine economy is underpinned by the doctrine of the *anakephalaiosis* according to which Christ repeats the story of Adam and thereby realizes the image of God that Adam in his immaturity forfeited.[18]

2. An equally important insight arose from the rejection of Modalism which either collapsed the Son and Spirit into the Father and possibly had to speak of the self-generation, self-crucifixion of the Father (Noëtus)[19] or interpreted Father, Son and Spirit as transitory modes of appearance of the one divine hypostasis, allegedly referred to as Son-Father (*huiopater*), as Sabellius is reported to have taught.[20] This rejection implied that the unity of the divine economy may not be conceived in such a way that it cancels out the ultimacy of God's particular self-identification as Father, Son and Spirit.

3. While Modalism and the insistence on the unity of the divine essence remained one of the characteristic emphases of Western theology, the particular danger of the Eastern tradition always appeared to be subordinationism. This, however, arose from the important conceptual proposal to speak of the Son (and in many cases of the Spirit) as a distinct hypostasis. One of the

[17] Cf. *Adversus haereses* IV, 20,1.
[18] Cf. *Adv. haer.* V, 16, 2f.; *Epideix.* 32–34.
[19] Cf. Hippolytus, *Contr. Noët.* I.
[20] Cf. Epiphanius, *Haer.* LXII, 1.

truly tragic cases of doctrinal history here is, in my view, Origen, who rightly insisted that Christian faith had to be presented as a comprehensive view of reality grounded in the relationship of Father, Logos and Spirit, who even suggested the formula of 'eternal generation' to designate the relationship of Father and Son,[21] and who was condemned for his subordinationism, precisely with the aid of the formula he had first introduced.

4. The trinitarian theologies of the origenist school which developed the Christian view of God and reality in the imagery of a cataract from the transcendent Oneness of God, the Father, over the mediating *hypostaseis* of the Logos and the Spirit to the immanence of the Many of creation, provoked the question that fuelled the Arian debate: where does the Divine end and the created start, does the Logos-Son belong to the unoriginated creator or to the originated and inferior order of creation? It is the necessity of coming to an ontological clarification of this question that constitutes the permanent significance of these debates for Christian theology, and it is the perennial achievement of the Council of Nicaea to have provided an answer to this question that opened up the road for the further explication of trinitarian doctrine.[22] This answer is summarized in the 'homoousios formula' for the explication of the relationship of the Father and the Son. However, this formula seemed to appear on the stage of doctrinal debate rather as an accident. It was only recognized in its full significance years after the Council and found acknowledgement under such confusions that one feels tempted to explain its ultimate success with the phrase *hominum confusione –Dei providentia*. What it states is that the relations between the Father and the Son (and as was later maintained against the Macedonian school of the *Pneumatomachoi*, between the Father, the Son and the Spirit) are internal relations in God's being and not external to the being of God. While this represented critically a clear rejection of Arianism – the Son belongs to God's being and not to the created realm – its constructive impact was far less clear and could only be slowly explicated in the complex exchanges between the different

---

[21] Cf. *Comm. in Jo.* XX. 18.

[22] Cf. now the exhaustive account of R. P. C. Hanson, *The Search for the Christian Doctrine of God*, Edinburgh: T & T Clark 1988.

parties of East and West after AD 350.[23]

It is the achievement of the Cappadocians that they provided a theological ontology for the trinitarian logic of Christian faith which found its classic expression in the formula *treis hypostaseis – mia ousia*. This, however, required an ontological innovation which has to be recognized, if one wants to make sense of their proposal. Their revolutionary suggestion was to distinguish between hypostasis and ousia and to find a new definition of hypostasis as person.[24] As is well known, both concepts had before been used interchangeably, both oscillating intensionally between individual essence and generic essence. The need for a new understanding of hypostasis can be clearly seen, if one attempts to explain the hypostasis in terms of the two fundamental ontological concepts which dominated Greek thought from Aristotle onwards: substance (*ousia*) and accident (*symbebekos*). If we interpret *hypostasis* in the sense of *ousia*, we must adopt some form of subordinationism, if we want to avoid tritheism, but this contradicts the character of the relatedness of Father, Son and Spirit in the trinitarian logic of Christian faith. If, however, we interpret Father, Son and Spirit as accidental properties of the divine *ousia* we are back to the unipersonalist views of Sabellianism. The revolutionary move of the Cappadocians was to introduce the concept of *hypostasis* as a logically and ontologically primitive concept, and to claim that it had theological priority for the talk of God in Christian faith. In Christian discourse about God the *hypostaseis* come first. To talk of the God Christians worship means to talk of the Father, the Son and the Spirit in their personal particularity which is identified precisely by their free relations to one another. These relations determine the personal particularity of Father, Son and Spirit as (in the terminology of Gregory

---

[23] For an excellent, brief and comprehensive account of the debate cf. Karlmann Beyschlag, *Grundriß der Dogmengeschichte, vol. I Gott und Welt*, Darmstadt: Wissenschaftliche Buchgesellschaft 1982, pp. 231–77.

[24] Cf. e.g. Basil, *Ep.* CCX, 5 and *Ep.* CCXXVI, 6. The revolutionary character of this ontological redefinition of the concept is programmatically developed by John D. Zizioulas, *Being as Communion. Studies in Personhood and the Church*, Crestwood, NY: St. Vladimir's Seminary Press 1985 (1993), esp. pp. 36ff, cf. also his article 'On Being a Person. Towards an Ontology of Personhood', in Chr. Schwöbel and C. E. Gunton (eds.), *Persons: Divine and Human*, Edinburgh: T & T Clark 1991, pp. 37ff, see also his contribution to this volume, pp. 44–60.

Nazianzen)[25] *agennesia* for the Father, *gennesis* for the Son and *ekporeusis* for the Spirit.

In their trinitarian theology the Cappadocians could over-come the antinomies of earlier trinitarian reflection by intro-ducing a conceptuality which reflects the trinitarian logic of Christian faith:

1. The unity of the divine economy can be seen as rooted in the triune being of God, but neither in the sense that it presents successive appearances of the one essence of God (as in Mod-alism), nor in the sense that the absolute Oneness of God is mediated through inferior divine beings (as in subordinationist theories). The divine economy has unity insofar as it is grounded in the relational unity of the communion of the persons of the Father, the Son and the Spirit.

2. To speak of God as the communion of the persons of the Father, the Son and the Spirit where each person is constituted in its personal particularity relationally through its relation to the other implies seeing these relations as internal relations, internal to the being of God. To be is for God to be the Father, the Son and the Spirit, to be a communion of persons. Being is there-fore always relational. This is indeed a revolution in ontology since it redefines on the basis of earlier Athanasian insights the concept of being as relational being.[26] This applies to the being of God as well as to created being, however with the important difference, that God's relational being is constitutive both for the being and for the relationality of created being. Apart from its relation to God created being has no being, nor can it be fully relational. To mention just one implication of this ontological revolution: The statement 'God is love' has no longer to be inter-preted in the sense of predicating a property or and attitude or a disposition to God's being. It can now be understood as an onto-logical statement about the mode of God's personal being in re-lation, and in this way love, interpreted on strictly relational terms, can be understood ontologically.

---

[25] Gregory Naz., *Or. theol.* 31, 10. Further material can be found in Karl Holl, *Amphilochius von Ikonium in seinem Verhältnis zu den großen Kappadoziern*, Tübingen 1904 (repr. 1969), pp. 159f. For different terminological suggestions by Basil, Gregory of Nyssa and Amphilochius cf. the comparison by Friedrich Loofs, *Leitfaden zum Studium der Dogmengeschichte*, 7th ed. by Kurt Aland, 1968, p. 203.

[26] The continuity between Athanasius and the Cappadocians is especially emphasized in F. Dinsen, *Homousios. Die Geschichte des Begriffs bis zum Konzil von Konstantinopel*, Diss. theol., Kiel 1977, esp. pp. 165ff.

There are differences in the ways the Cappadocians expounded their ontological discovery, there are various ways in which their conception was further developed in Eastern theology, and there are divergent systematic reconstructions of the Cappadocians' thought today. Recognition of the revolutionary character of their ontological discovery does not necessarily commit us to accept any one of these expositions of their thought uncritically. It does, however, entail the acknowledgement that we have in their work the most significant attempt in patristic thought to provide a coherent ontology for the trinitarian logic of Christian faith – an attempt which we ignore at our peril.

The implications of the Cappadocian clarification of the doctrine of the Trinity for Christology are immense. By excluding modalist and subordinationist interpretations of the Son and by denying the adjectival use of 'God' as a predicate, it defined the way in which the christological question could be raised. It could now be approached in the form: In what sense can we say that the incarnate Christ is God the Son, the second person of the Trinity? By phrasing the christological question in this way, it can also be indicated in what sense the clarification of trinitarian doctrine also raises a whole cluster of christological problems which can be summarized in the question: If the incarnate Christ is the Son, the second person of the Trinity, in what sense can we assert his true humanity? The fact that these questions should by no means be seen as purely speculative metaphysical riddles, is indicated by the two soteriological principles determining the range of answers which could be seen as appropriate: the principle 'only God can save' which expresses the sole agency of God in salvation, and the principle 'The unassumed is the unhealed' which safeguards the reality of the Incarnation.[27] It would be a mistake to interpret both principles as the premises of a deductive argument. Rather, they are summary expressions encapsulating the central content of the Gospel narrative and of the Christian kerygma: Salvation as it is proclaimed in the message of Jesus' life, death and resurrection is exclusively a divine work which is enacted through the Son's participation in the reality of a human life as it is portrayed in the Gospel narratives.

---

[27] On the function of these principles cf. M. Wiles, 'The Unassumed is the Unhealed', in *Working Papers in Doctrine*, London: SCM Press 1976, pp. 108–21.

Viewed from our perspective, it appears that there is a difference between the clarification of the doctrine of the Trinity at Nicaea and Constantinople and the development of christological thought which received its normative criteria at Chalcedon. With regard to trinitarian theology it could be said that the Cappadocians turned the criticism of inadequate conceptions of the relationship of Father, Son and Spirit into a constructive proposal which creatively transcended the antinomies from which it started. In Christology it seems that the rejection of inadequate answers to the central christological questions did not advance beyond the critical stage where criteria were asserted which could exclude inadequate conceptions but did not directly suggest a constructive solution to the problems indicated by the complementary heresies of 'Eutychianism' and 'Nestorianism'.

The conceptual expressions of the Chalcedonian Definition succeed in stating the necessary conditions for a christological conception by asserting the unity of the person of Christ and by insisting that his being perfect in Godhead and perfect in manhood is to be acknowledged in two natures, without confusion, without change, without division, without separation. The relation of these criteria to the fundamental assertions of the doctrine of the Trinity is clearly expressed in the assertion that these statements are made about 'one and the same Son'. However, the Definition does not indicate in which way these criteria can be applied to formulate a coherent christological conception. This limitation of the Chalcedonian Definition is witnessed by the fact that historically it ended one series of christological debates and inaugurated another. Throughout the history of doctrine Chalcedon has amply proved its critical capacity in excluding inadequate conceptions of the Incarnation, its constructive potential only became apparent occasionally where its christological criteria were firmly set against the background of the trinitarian understanding of God – perhaps most notably in the work of Maximus Confessor.[28]

This state of affairs had very serious implications when the doctrine of the Trinity was reinterpreted in the West in the

---

[28] Cf. François-Marie Léthel, *Théologie de l'agonie du Christ. La liberté humaine du Fils de Dieu et son importance sotériologique mises en lumière par saint Maxime le Confesseur*, Paris 1979.

conceptuality of Augustine's trinitarianism which for most of the history of Western theology shaped its understanding of the triune God. The effects of Augustine's reinterpretation of the Cappadocian theology of the Trinity has been much investigated and criticized in recent systematic theology.[29] It may suffice to repeat a few of the main points of this critical assessment. It is pointed out that while the Cappadocians approached trinitarian reflection from the concept of the person, emphasizing the personal particularity and relational unity of the trinitarian persons, Augustine's approach centres on the non-relational unity of the divine essence, which immediately renders the concept of the person a mystery.[30] The attempt at giving it meaning by means of the analogical appropriation of the immanent relations of mental acts of one subject, has the effect of transforming the relations of the trinitarian persons into the relational structure of one divine consciousness. The upshot of these developments has been characterized as an internalization and intellectualization of trinitarian language. The effects of this modification are most apparent in its application to the understanding of divine agency. The Cappadocian axiom[31] that the three persons of the Trinity always act in communion, is now understood in terms of the uniformity of divine action. The slogan *opera trinitatis ad extra sunt indivisa*[32] implies the danger of making the doctrine of the Trinity irrelevant for the divine economy and of introducing a rift between the immanent activities of the trinitarian persons and God's action in relation to the created order. The separation of the doctrine of the one God (De Deo Uno) and the doctrine of the Trinity (De Deo Trino)[33] and the relegation of the doctrine of the Trinity to the realms of speculation, worship and spirituality is only the logical outcome of the reinterpretation of trinitarian language in Augustine and the Augustinian tradition. There has always been more to Augustine's trinitarian thought, most nota-

---

[29] Cf. Colin Gunton, *The Promise of Trinitarian Theology*, Edinburgh: T & T Clark 1991, ch. 3. Cf. also R. W. Jenson, 'The Triune God', pp. 140ff.
[30] Cf. Augustine, *De Trin.* V, 9, 10.
[31] Cf. e.g. Gregor. Naz., *Or. theol.* IV.
[32] This phrase is not found in Augustine although he speaks of the inseparability of divine action: *De Trin.* I, 4, 7: *inseparabiliter operentur*.
[33] The effects of this division have been classically illustrated in Karl Rahner, *The Trinity*, Eng. trans. J. Donceel, New York: Herder & Herder 1970.

bly perhaps his creative employment of the analogy of love for the interpretation of the Trinity,[34] and it has to be emphasized that this is one of the major stimuli for the creative developments in Western trinitarian reflection, as, for instance, in Richard of St Victor's conceptual reconstruction of the doctrine of the Trinity.[35]

However, what became normative in Western theology, firmly established in the canon of the medieval text-book tradition, is the separation of the dogmatic treatment of God and the divine attributes from the doctrine of the Trinity and the interpretation of the unity of God's trinitarian agency *ad extra* as uniformity, which excludes functional differentiation.[36] The upshot of this for Christology is, in my view, at the root of the modern christological crisis. Christological thought lost its trinitarian framework and the ontology of personhood discovered and expounded by the Cappadocians was replaced by different conceptions of personhood which in many cases treated the concept of the person not as a logically and ontologically primitive concept. Christology could now be understood as the doctrine of the two natures. 'How could God become man while retaining his true divinity and assuming full humanity?' becomes a standard form of the christological question. Furthermore, since the being and the attributes of the one God were defined apart from trinitarian reflection on the persons, the divine nature was at least partly conceived in a sense which owes much to the considerations of natural theology understood as the praeambula fidei. The divine nature is seen as defined by the attributes of omniscience, omnipotence, omnipresence and eternity (interpreted as atemporality). With regard to the conception of the human nature a non-christological conception becomes dominant where not the humanity of Christ is seen as the paradigm of what it means to be human, but the kind-essence of human nature as it was exemplified in Adam in *statu integretatis*.

Isolated from the trinitarian logic of Christian faith and its ontological explication in the doctrine of the Trinity the christological problems become almost intractable, a formidable chal-

---

[34] Cf. *De Trin.* IX, 2ff. and XV, 6 & 17–19.

[35] Cf. F. Courth, Trinität in der Scholastik, *Handbuch der Dogmengeschichte* II/1b, Freiburg: Herder 1985, pp. 63–8.

[36] Cf. Robert W. Jenson, 'The Holy Spirit', in Carl E. Braaten and Robert W. Jenson (eds.), *Christian Dogmatics*, vol. II, pp. 101–78, esp. pp. 126f.

lenge for logicians and metaphysicians and a breeding-ground for paradox. Approached from the logical and ontological opposition of the two natures of divinity and humanity, it oscillates throughout the history of Western Christianity between a 'unification'-Christology tending towards Eutychianism and 'disjunction'-Christology leaning towards Nestorianism as long as christological reflection is conducted within the criteriological framework of the Chalcedonian definition.[37] Once this framework is no longer accepted as defining the boundaries of the christological task, the dualism of time and eternity, of spirit and matter and of the necessary and the contingent which threatens theological thought once the trinitarian logic of Christian faith and its ontological implications are ignored, leads modern Christology into the antinomies which characterize its modern crisis. The neglect of the trinitarian framework for Christology also generates the disjunction of Christology and soteriology which is so forcefully expressed in Melanchthon's protest against Christology as metaphysical speculation. The displacement of the concept of the person in Christology which is an implication of the neglect of the trinitarian framework of Christology leads to a de-personalization of soteriology which is consequently developed in apersonal models of legal exchanges. The exploration of the *anamnesis* of the patient seems to provide extensive evidence for our diagnosis that the trinitarian 'forgetfulness' of Western theology is intrinsically linked to the critical state of modern Christology.

IV. From Diagnosis to Therapy: Some Suggestions

When we now turn from diagnosis to therapeutic suggestions, it has to be said immediately that the ills of modern Christology are unlikely to be overcome by a miraculous wonder drug which theologians could prescribe to effect immediate recovery. The state of the patient rather requires the careful consideration of tentative proposals which might indicate possibilities of overcoming the present state of crisis. Consultation about the best possible course of treatment is needed, and perhaps even respon-

---

[37] This has been aptly demonstrated by W. Pannenberg, *Grundzüge der Christologie*, pp. 291–334.

sible theological experimentation to indicate the changes that
the crisis necessitates. The proposal I want to make does not come
as a surprise. It consists in the attempt at restoring the background of trinitarian reflection to Christology, to reintegrate
Christology into the framework of the trinitarian logic of
Christian faith. What is required – and this task can only be
hinted at here – is a trinitarian hermeneutic for Christology.

1. The attempt at developing a trinitarian hermeneutic for
Christology has immediate implications for the understanding
of the task of Christology and the approach to this task.
Developed from within the framework of the trinitarian logic of
Christian faith, the task of Christology cannot be conceived as
establishing the divinity of Jesus Christ by rational argument or
historical proof. It should rather be interpreted as the conceptual reconstruction of the truth claims concerning the person and
work of Jesus Christ asserted, presupposed and implied in
Christian faith as it is practised in worship, proclamation,
confession and the Christian life. Christology of reflection
already presupposes the Christology of witness and attempts to
give it a coherent conceptual expression.

Understanding the task of Christology in systematic theology as
one of conceptual reconstruction of the primary expressions of
faith in Christ in worship and proclamation is not only a methodological stratagem, it also reflects the starting-point and context of christological reflection. If the task of Christology is
perceived from the perspective of an approach 'from above' or
'from below', from the historical Jesus or from the Christus
praesens or from the being or the significance of Christ this is
already an abstraction from the life of the Christian community
where christological confession has its immediate context. By
approaching the task of reflective Christology from the life of
the Christian community where Christ is acclaimed, professed
and proclaimed Christology starts from within the community
which sees itself as part of the divine economy in that it
celebrates the trinitarian being of God as the condition for its
own being and acknowledges its participation in the life of the
triune God by grace in its witness and eucharistic practice. At the
same time this community distinguishes itself from the trinitarian life of God precisely in its worship and proclamation in
witnessing to God, Father, Son and Spirit as the ground of all
being, meaning and truth as the source, the agent and the reality

of salvation. Seeing the Christian community as the starting-point of Christology means to locate the enterprise of doing Christology already in the relations which are constituted in the divine economy where the Spirit makes believers copresent to Christ and Christ copresent to the believers so that they participate in this way by God's unconditional grace as Christ's brothers and sisters in his relationship with the Father. The point of Christology becomes apparent where it is acknowledged that what happens intra muros ecclesiae concerns the world and that the Christian Gospel claims to present the truth of salvation for the whole of creation.

2. Developing a trinitarian hermeneutic for Christology not only implies relocating Christology in the life of the Christian community whose existence is part of the divine economy, it also seems to suggest quite far-reaching changes in the conceptuality of Christology. Doing Christology within the framework of the trinitarian logic of Christian faith requires a paradigm shift from natures to persons. This implies that the question of the divinity of Christ should not be interpreted in terms of his possession of a divine nature, but should primarily be seen in terms of his relationship as the Son to the Father as it is mediated through the Spirit. Consequently, the question of the humanity of Christ should not be interpreted as the possession of a human nature, but as the way in which the true destiny of humanity is actualized in the life, death and resurrection of Christ. Locating the question of the divinity of Christ in the description of the relationship of the Father to the Son through the Spirit and of the Son through the Spirit to the Father brings a radical change to the understanding of the divinity of Christ. Christ is not divine because he possesses a divine nature, but because God the Father relates to him in the Spirit as the Son and thereby distinguishes himself as the Father from the Son and in this way is in personal communion with the Son in the Spirit. Conversely, Christ is divine in relating to God the Father in the Spirit and thereby distinguishing himself as the Son from the Father and in this way is in personal communion with the Father and the Spirit. The question of the divinity of Christ is therefore to be interpreted strictly as the question of the divinity of the incarnate Son.

This paradigm shift from natures to persons which seems to me to be the heart of a trinitarian hermeneutic for Christology

has important repercussions for the conception of the doctrine of
the Trinity. It requires that the rigid distinction between the
processions in the immanent Trinity and the missions in the
economic Trinity is abandoned and replaced by a description of
the trinitarian relations which integrates both the personal
distinction and personal communion of Father, Son and Spirit.
Wolfhart Pannenberg has summarized this change by stating:

> The Father does not merely beget the Son, but also hands over his
> kingdom to him and receives it back from him. The Son is not only
> begotten, but he is also obedient to him and thereby glorifies him as
> the one God. The Spirit is not only breathed. He also fills the Son
> and glorifies him in his obedience to the Father, thereby glorifying
> the Father himself. In so doing he leads into all truth (John 16, 13)
> and searches out the deep things of Godhead (1 Cor. 2, 10f.).[38]

Pannenberg's statement highlights the changes that are
introduced into the doctrine of the Trinity, once the rigid
distinction between 'processions' and 'missions' is abandoned.
This immediately implies giving up the restrictive view of the
trinitarian relations exclusively as originating relations, and
seeing them as mutual and reciprocal relations, though of course
not as symmetrical relations. The mutuality of the trinitarian
persons, includes both their personal constitution in relation to
one another and their personal distinction from one another. As
Pannenberg's phrases indicate, this also restores the biblical
language of the trinitarian logic of Christian faith to the
ontology of the doctrine of the Trinity.

If we accept that the *locus* of the divinity of Christ is not the
possession of a divine nature, but the relationship of Sonship to
God the Father mediated in the Spirit, then the further question
is not how the possession of a divine nature is compatible with
the possession of a human nature, but how this relationship of
Sonship can be exercised and enacted in the reality of a human
life. It is at this point that the significance of the Gospel narratives becomes evident for a trinitarian Christology. They
present from different perspectives and in different theological
interpretations the story of Jesus as the story of a life constituted
by and conducted in the Spirit which is obedient to God the
Father to the death on Calvary and to the resurrection on the

---

[38] W. Pannenberg, *Systematic Theology*, vol. I, Edinburgh: T & T Clark
1992, p. 320.

third day and which in this way is the coming of God's Kingdom for the salvation of his creation. One element of this story is here of special significance. The obedience of Jesus as the Son to the Father is over and over again from his birth to his resurrection described as one that is enabled from the Father by the Spirit and exercised in response to the Father in the Spirit. Trinitarian Christology is always pneumatological Christology and vice versa. The claim of the Christian message is that in Jesus Christ the Son becomes history so that the eschatological promise of God's community with his creation becomes a reality which incorporates the history of creation. The Christ event is therefore the historical enactment of Sonship in relation to the Father and exercised through the Spirit as the reality of reconciliation between God and his alienated creation. The task of a trinitarian Christology is to show that divine Sonship can be enacted in the historical reality of a human life without reducing it to a mere illustration or a transitory appearance of Sonship.

3. The paradigm shift from natures to persons, from substance metaphysics to a metaphysics of relations, has similar implications for the understanding of the humanity of Christ. From this perspective to be human does not mean possessing a human nature, but to be a person, to actualize the relational being of humanity in becoming a person in relation to other persons. The statement that Christ is truly human is in the context of Christian faith in Christ not simply to be interpreted as the assertion that his humanity is to be seen as participation in the factual state of human existence after the Fall. Rather, it should be seen as the new humanity of the second Adam, in whom the created destiny of human being to be in relation to God is actualized. Interpreting Christ's humanity simply in terms of the instantiation of the kind-essence of humanity deprives the doctrine of the person of Christ of its soteriological point. This consists in the promise of the Gospel that in him humanity is restored to its created destiny, recreated as the eschatological reality of being in which the effects of the Fall, of the estrangement of humanity from their creator, is overcome, not only in his humanity, but also for ours insofar as we participate by grace through the Spirit in his relationship to the Father. The recreation of humanity in Christ is in the imagery of biblical language expressed as the restoration of the *imago Dei* in the image of the Son. Here the

effects of a trinitarian hermeneutic for Christology lead to particularly interesting results. If to be created in the image of God is – as Colin Gunton has suggested[39] – to be called to be persons in communion, a communion which includes personal freedom and personal particularity, and if this destiny is to be realized in dependence of the human creature on God, then the Fall is to be understood as the rebellion of human beings against their created destiny: to be persons in relation and in dependence on their triune creator. The effect of the Fall could then be seen as the *dislocation* of human beings in the network of relationships in which they are created, and this dislocation finds its most significant expression in the attempt of human beings at realizing their personhood by implicitly or explicitly denying the condition of its possibility in the relation of the triune creator to humanity.[40] If the humanity of Christ is to be seen as the recreation of true humanity as the fulfilment of the relational existence of human being in dependence on the triune God, it is therefore required for Christology to show that in Christ true humanity is constituted through its relation to the triune God and exercised in the acknowledgement of this dependence in the relational existence of human being.

4. This is, in my view, precisely the point of the classical doctrine that the humanity of Christ subsists *enhypostatically* in the person of the Son and is therefore anhypostatic, has no *hypostasis* of its own. This doctrine states that the true humanity of Christ as the recreation of the created destiny of human beings to be persons in relation is constituted through its assumption by the person of the Son. Only in this hypostatic relation to the Son is the humanity of Christ the recreation of the relational being of humanity. Conversely, it is only in being the hypostasis of the humanity of Christ that the divine Son is the incarnate Son. The identity of Jesus Christ can therefore only be described as the union of the person of the Son who is constituted as the Son through his relation to the Father in the Spirit with the humanity of Jesus which is constituted in its relational

---

[39] Cf. C. E. Gunton, 'Trinity, Ontology and Anthropology: Towards a Renewal of the Doctrine of the *Imago Dei*', in Chr. Schwöbel and C. E. Gunton (eds.), *Persons: Divine and Human*, pp. 47–61.

[40] Cf. my paper 'Human Being as Relational Being. Twelve Theses for a Christian Anthropology', in Schwöbel and Gunton (eds.), *Persons*, pp. 141–65.

structure precisely through its hypostatic participation in the person of the Son in its relations to the Father and the Spirit. These statements are, however, only conceptual reconstructions of the life in which this identity finds its expression in a life-story. Identity descriptions as attempts to answer the question 'Who is this?' have in contrast to classification statements which answer the question 'What is this?' always a narrative form. The christological question 'Who is Jesus Christ?' is therefore not answered by abstract metaphysical statements, but by the telling of a story: the story of the life, death and re-surrection of Jesus Christ as the one to whom God the Father relates through the Spirit as the Son and who relates to God the Father in the Spirit.

5. A Christology which is developed on the basis of the trinitarian hermeneutic of Christian faith, and presents the relationship of the Son to the Father in the Spirit as the *locus* of the divinity of Christ and the recreation of true humanity in Christ through its hypostatic union with the person of the Son as the locus of his humanity, attempts to give an account of the identity of Christ as the incarnate Son whose being is to be in two sets of relationships: the trinitarian relations of Father, Son and Spirit and the relational being of humanity. It is at this point where we speak of two 'sets of relationships' that what the language of the two natures intended to express makes a re-appearance in a trinitarian Christology. The Chalcedonian criteria (that the divinity and the humanity of Christ in the hypostatic union are related without confusion, without change, without division, without separation) have an important critical function for the project of a trinitarian Christology. They safeguard the distinction between the being of the creator and created being. The eternal is not simply temporalized in the hypostatic union, neither is the temporal eternalized, nor do they co-exist in unrelated division and separation. The relation-ship between the Father, the Son and the Spirit is eternal, even though the incarnate Son relates to the Father in the Spirit in the created temporality of a human life. Conversely, Christ re-lates as the Son to the Father in the Spirit in the Incarnation in the temporal reality of a human life, and this is not denied in asserting that this relationship is eternally the relationship of the Son to the Father in the Spirit. The eternal life of God the creator is disclosed in the reality of the very stuff of creation

which is thereby not destroyed, but exalted by grace into the communion of the divine persons. Although the distinction between divinity and humanity is preserved, humanity as temporal, created existence is brought into the hypostatic union of the person of the Son. *Infinitum capax finiti* is the principle which determines this union which is a true hypostatic relation, incorporating distinction, and not just a fusion or the co-existence of two natures.

6. This understanding of Jesus Christ as the one person of the incarnate Son who exists in two relationships (the relations to God the Father and the Spirit, which are constitutive for his divinity as the Son; and the relations of human being as created relational existence which finds the fulfilment of its destiny in the relationship of God's daughters and sons through the Son and the Spirit to the Father) would be incomplete if its soteriological implications remained implicit. Two points need to be made here. The soteriological relevance of the Christ-event which is presented in this way is not something that would have to be added to this ontological account of the person of Christ. Rather, it becomes apparent when the person of Christ is not merely described in its ontological constitution, but when this ontological account is presented in the narrative identity description of Jesus Christ. The traditional account of the offices of Christ as Prophet, Priest and King are therefore to be interpreted as explications of aspects of the enactment of the identity of Christ in history which presuppose the twofold relational structure of his being: that in him God relates to his alienated creation in disclosing his will, actualizing his righteousness and bringing about his Kingdom; and that in him humanity relates to the triune God by becoming obedient to the will of the Father, by sacrificing its futile attempt at personal self-constitution and by actively acknowledging the Kingdom as the ultimate purpose of God's community with humanity.

The second point concerning the soteriological implications of the being of the person of Christ is perhaps the most significant for establishing theologically the unity of Christology and soteriology. It is the conviction of Christian faith that the enhypostatic being of the Son is the eschatological promise for the whole of creation, that the personal being of the Son is the paradigm for the reconciled being of the whole of creation, the ground of its possibility and the mode in which it becomes actual. To put it as bluntly as possible: The Kingdom of God is the enhypostatic life of the whole of creation in communion with the triune creator, so that the personal being-in-communion which God eternally is, is the ultimate eschatological reality for the whole of creation – to be in communion with God without change, without fusion, without division and without separation. This eschatological reality is there in the person of Christ as the *autobasileia*, the Kingdom in his person. It is actualized where the Holy Spirit makes the believing community copresent with the Son and thereby relates it to the Father so that God's will of love, which is rooted in his triune being, is ultimately victorious in the Kingdom of God as the communion of love between God and the creation.

Our steps from description of the symptoms and diagnosis to suggestions for the therapy of the ills of Christology has led us to the point where we have to make a modest and very tentative prognosis. It consists in the prediction that the chances of recovery for Christology are higher if it accepts the treatment of a trinitarian hermeneutic for Christology, than if it continues to pursue the activity of doing Christology from the antinomies which characterize Christology's modern crisis. But perhaps it is also necessary to add a word of caution. Developing a Christology within the framework of the trinitarian logic of God has side-effects which seriously change established modes of reflection in Christian theology. It will be necessary to understand God, his being and attributes no longer from the simple contrast of created being and the being of the creator, but from the point in history where this contrast has been bridged in the enhypostatic being of Christ which is the promise for the fulfilment of the eschatological being of the whole of creation. This implies seeing the life, death and resurrection of Jesus Christ not as the *Kenosis* of the attributes of God, but as their *Plerosis* in the person of the Son. Discourse about the being and attributes of God is not the presupposition of a trinitarian account of the person and work of Christ, but one of its results.

V. Brief Unscientific Postscript

In view of the seriousness of the modern christological crisis, and faced with the fragmentary and limited character of theological reflection attempting to overcome it, the prospects of a full recovery would seem decidedly gloomy, if the healing process had to come exclusively from theological thought. Perhaps it is a necessary reminder for theologians that the true resources for overcoming the crisis of Christology are to be found in the scriptural witness and the worship of the Christian community of faith whose life is a far more promising sign of hope than theological thought could ever be.

7. The Eschatological Roots of the Doctrine of the Trinity

Ingolf U. Dalferth

One of the prominent features of twentieth century theology is the recovery of the eschatological dimension. And one of the remarkable facts about theology in this century is the renaissance of the doctrine of the Trinity. A decade ago it was still possible to bewail the 'relative neglect of the doctrine of the Trinity'[1] and to suggest, somewhat along Schleiermacher's lines, that this doctrine still waits for its theological recovery in terms intelligible to our time. Today, after dozens of books and articles on the Trinity, we may still wonder about its intelligibility, but we can hardly speak of neglect any more. On the contrary, the conviction that 'the doctrine of the Trinity simply *is* the Christian doctrine of God'[2] seems to be one of the least contentious claims among Christian theologians today. Nicholas Lash speaks the mind of many when he claims that 'any doctrine of God which has ceased to be trinitarian in character has thereby ceased to be Christian'.[3] What he fails to provide, however, are reasons as to why this should be so. Yet this we must do if we want to render the doctrine of the Trinity intelligible to our time.

There are various reasons which one could mention. But the central reason, I suggest, is that only a trinitarian account of God is true to the foundational experience of the Christian faith: the experience of the eschatological reality of the risen Christ. I do not claim this to be a very original view. I only think that it is true. But since, as I am well aware, not all will agree it may not be entirely besides the point to elaborate more fully why and in which way the eschatological experience of the Christian faith requires a trinitarian account of God.

---

[1] J. Mackey, *The Christian Experience of God as Trinity*, London: SCM Press 1983, p. 3.
[2] N. Lash, 'Considering the Trinity', *Modern Theology* 2, 1986, pp. 183–96, p. 183
[3] Ibid.

I.

Discussions of the Trinity in the past decade have been numerous and wide-ranging, and I shall not even attempt to summarize them here. For our purposes it is enough to remind you of the range of views that have been proposed. Since I have to be selective, I shall concentrate on some contemporary Protestant theologians from Germany. Not merely because I am German, Protestant and a theologian but because, to quote Nicholas Lash once again, 'it was primarily in German thought that what might be called the "post-history" of the doctrine of the Trinity was worked out' whereas 'in the English-speaking world . . . , with renewed vigour in recent years, the underlying assumptions of eighteenth-century theism have dictated the terms of debate concerning the question of God'.[4]

What cannot be contentious is that most recent discussions of the Trinity start from the trinitarian theologies of Barth and Rahner. Both of them reacted to the widespread neglect of the doctrine of the Trinity in Western theology at their time. Few denied that it was one of the principal 'mysteries of faith'. But it was of little practical significance to the life of faith. Since Augustine and scholastic Augustinianism, trinitarian thought had come to wear an abstract air, and the Western inclination towards a unitarian formulation of the doctrine of God was even further increased by the Enlightenment. Where the doctrine of the Trinity was not held on merely traditionalist grounds, it was discarded altogether or it took on a speculative life of its own.

According to Karl Rahner, the first decisive move in the isolation and subsequent sterilization of the doctrine of the Trinity was the separation of the discussion of 'the one God' from the discussion of 'the triune God'. The doctrine of the Trinity became a doctrine alongside others rather than the frame of reference or the grammar of all the others. The Reformation did not achieve a restoration of trinitarian thought; and at the beginning of the nineteenth century Schleiermacher rightly observed that to achieve this was still one of the unfulfilled tasks of Protestant theology. However, the problem was not merely a Protestant one. Since the Enlightenment discussions of the Trinity have

---

[4] Op. cit., p. 185.

become subordinated to preoccupation with the unitary being of
God. Philosophical theism – the belief in the existence of a supreme and beneficent Being – was widely taken over by Christian theologians. Nineteenth century attempts to defend trinitarian thought against these developments led to its absorption
into the discussion of the being of God as Absolute where it took
on a speculative life on its own. But this estranged it even further
from the life of the church. It left the figurative language of
faith without adequate conceptual form. And it opened up a gap
between the life of faith and the intellectual engagement with
the problem of God.

Philosophers were first to react against these developments.
With Feuerbach, Marx, Freud and Nietzsche the speculative
movement and its attempted rescue of trinitarian thought came
under vigorous attack. Yet since its close association with the
Christian tradition had made its vulnerability, the vulnerability of Christian theology as well, the criticism of these thinkers
was largely unacceptable to (liberal) theology. Only when, in
our century, theology gradually began to divorce itself from Enlightenment theism and its aftermath, it could critically come to
grips with both, the speculative tradition and its critics Marx,
Freud and Nietzsche by taking a vigorously trinitarian and explicitly anti-theistic approach.

Anti-theism, then, i.e. the rejection of Enlightenment theism,
its consequences and its antithesis (atheism), has been one of the
major motifs for trinitarian theology today. It is the common
denominator of such different theologies as those of Moltmann,
Jüngel, Pannenberg and Wagner. They all agree that Christian
theology, in order to move beyond the barren alternative of
theism and atheism, must be trinitarian in character. But they
differ widely and even irreconcilably in the ways in which they
ground their trinitarian positions. A few hints must suffice:

1. For Eberhard Jüngel,[5] as for Barth in his later years, the
doctrine of the Trinity is christologically grounded.[6] Originally

---

[5] J. B. Webster, *Eberhard Jüngel. An Introduction to his Theology*,
Cambridge: Cambrifge University Press 1986, gives a good account of
Jüngel's position.
[6] E. Jüngel, 'Das Verhältnis von "ökonomischer" und "immanenter" Trinität.
Erwägungen über eine biblische Begründung der Trinitätslehre – im
Anschluß an und in Auseinandersetzung mit Karl Rahners Lehre vom
dreifaltigen Gott als transzendentem Urgrund der Heilsgeschichte', in

Barth's doctrine of the Trinity was 'bound up with the concept of revelation, in the strict sense of God's self-revelation which is grounded in God's trinitarian self-unfolding'.[7] This invited the criticism that Barth's doctrine, by working out the structure and implication of the *Deus dixit*, 'is fashioned out of the logic of God as absolute subject'[8] and that his 'construal of the Trinity as the self-unfolding of a divine subject inevitably does damage to the co-eternity of the divine persons, diminishing their plurality to mere modes of being subordinate to the divine subject.'[9] But as the *Church Dogmatics* evolved, the emphasis shifted away from the inner structure of revelation towards the history of Jesus and, in particular, the cross. And in stressing the 'displacement' between Father and Son at the cross, Barth increasingly intensified the divine plurality.[10]

Jüngel criticizes Barth for not taking that process far enough. His own work on the Trinity starts from God's self-identification with the crucified at the cross, and he conceives its function as being to work out the identity of God's being-for-himself and his being-for-us in the person of Jesus Christ. If God has identified himself with the crucified one, we must 'distinguish God from God'.[11] But the unsurpassable contrast between Father and Son at the cross is not a 'contradiction within God'.[12] God – as Spirit – remains at the same time related to himself in this contrast. This is why we must give not merely a binitarian, but a trinitarian account of God. Jüngel follows a long tradition of Western

---

Entsprechungen: Gott – Wahrheit – Mensch, München 1980, pp. 265–75, p. 267f.

[7] W. Pannenberg, 'Die Subjektivität Gottes und die Trinitätslehre. Ein Beitrag zur Beziehung zwischen Karl Barth und der Philosophie Hegels', in *Grundfragen systematischer Theologie. Gesammelte Aufsätze II*, Göttingen 1980, pp. 96–111, p. 98.

[8] Webster, p. 74.

[9] W. Pannenberg, 'Der Gott der Geschichte. Der trinitarische Gott und die Wahrheit der Geschichte', in *Grundfragen systematischer Theologie. Gesammelte Aufsätze II*, Göttingen: Vandenhoeck & Ruprecht 1980, pp. 112–28, p. 124.

[10] Webster, op. cit., p. 75.

[11] E. Jüngel, 'Thesen zur Grundlegung der Theologie', in *Unterwegs zur Sache. Theologische Bemerkungen*, München: Chr. Kaiser Verlag 1972, pp. 274–95, p. 293.

[12] E. Jüngel, *God as the Mystery of the World. On the Foundation of the Theology of the Crucified One in the Dispute between Theism and Atheism*, Edinburgh: T & T Clark 1983, p. 346.

thought when he describes the Spirit as the reassertion of unity
after difference. But he has difficulty in articulating, with any
clarity, the personal agency of the Spirit.[13] So instead of press-
ing from the event of the cross towards an account of the Trinity
as an irreducibly plural society, he turns to working out the *unity*
of the self-differentiated God in terms of the concept of love:
Because God is love, he is essentially related, both in himself
and in the sense of being open to what is different from him. In
God 'to be' and 'to be related' are one and the same; and the character of the ontological relationality of God is love, i.e. – in
Jüngel's definition – 'the unity of life [self-relation] and death
[self-loss] in favour of life'.[14] Hence even in his self-abasement
at the cross God is not foreign to himself but eminently true to
himself: 'in giving himself away, he does not lose but becomes
himself'[15] because, as God, he does not simply *act lovingly* but
ontologically *is* love. Hence there is no need to posit 'an essence
of God behind his loving *pro nobis*, for his aseity takes form as
loving self-renunciation'.[16]

2. Jüngel uses the concepts of 'love' and 'relation' to retain the
coherence and unity of the divine being without sacrificing the
sense of 'displacement' which is introduced into the being of God
by the cross. Moltmann starts from the same Barthian legacy but
moves in a different direction. His case for the necessity of trinitarian discourse is developed from asserting God's real relation
to human pain and suffering, supremely exemplified by the cross.
At the cross, he says, God was abandoned by God. He not merely
holds, as Jüngel does, that the cross occasions the distinction
between God and God but understands the separation of Father
from Son in the dereliction of the cross in a full mythological
sense. He is able to do this because for him the divine self-sepa-
ration on the cross is grounded in the priority of persons over
relations and the repudiation of any reduction of the three
persons to the absolute subject as substance. For him, the primordial reality is the plurality of the persons, and '*the unity of
God is only actual in that plurality*'[17] So he develops his well-
known pluralist account of a social Trinity of Father, Son and

---

[13] Webster, op. cit., p. 77.
[14] Jüngel, *God as Mystery*, p. 299.
[15] Webster, op. cit., p. 72.
[16] Ibid.
[17] Pannenberg, 'Subjektivität Gottes', p. 108.

Spirit linked together only by what he calls the trinitarian history of God. That is to say, the Trinity itself is seen in terms of God's involvement in historical becoming, and although Moltmann goes so far as to deny a definite *taxis* between the persons 'in favour of a Trinity that can be taken "in any order", he nevertheless relates it to our progressive ordering towards a free, creative, relationship of "friendship" to God in the Holy Spirit'.[18] However, while this secures that God is not a closed monad, but a community of loving interaction open to a reality beyond itself, Moltmann so much stresses the personal agency of Father, Son and Spirit, that it becomes difficult to see how it still can be said to be one and the same God. Moreover, in his account of the separation of Father and Son at the cross he does not succeed, as he has acknowledged, in doing justice to the agency of the Spirit vis-à-vis Father and Son. He has attempted to remedy this recently by developing an account not only of the *kenosis* of the Son but also of the *kenosis* of the Spirit.[19] But this in fact increases his difficulties of distinguishing clearly between the agency of the Son and the Spirit and virtually bars him from ascribing to the Spirit not merely the function of demonstrating the openness of the triune community but also, as we saw in Jüngel, of establishing its unity by overcoming the difference between Father and Son.

3. Moltmann's difficulties with the unity of God are one reason for Wolfhart Pannenberg to look for a different solution.[20] He agrees with Jüngel and Moltmann that Barth's earlier attempt to develop the doctrine of the Trinity from the formal notion of revelation as expressed in the statement 'God reveals himself as the Lord' is unsatisfactory. Instead of starting from the formal notion of revelation, we must start from the content of God's revelation in Christ. But for Pannenberg this is not so much the cross and the relationship between Father, Son and Spirit in

---

[18] J. Milbank, 'The Second Difference: For a Trinitarianism without Reserve', *Modern Theology* 2, 1986, pp. 213–34, p. 223.

[19] D. L. Dabney, *Die Kenosis des Geistes: Kontinuität zwischen Schöpfung und Erlösung im Werk des Heiligen Geistes*, unpublished doctoral diss., Tübingen 1989; H. H. Lin, *Die Person des Heiligen Geistes als Thema der Pneumatologie in der reformierten Theologie*, unpublished doctoral diss., Tübingen 1990.

[20] The following relies on the excellent account of Pannenberg's position by Chr. Schwöbel, 'Wolfhart Pannenberg', in D. F. Ford (ed.), *The Modern Theologians. An Introduction to Christian Theology in the Twentieth Century*, vol. I, Oxford: Blackwell 1990, pp. 257–92.

terms of which the cross can be understood as a salvific and revelatory event. Rather it is the particular relationship of the historical Jesus to God and, in particular, the fact that Jesus distinguished himself clearly from the God he called Father and, in renouncing himself completely, made room for the action of the Father and the coming of his kingdom. If this is interpreted, as Pannenberg does, as the self-revelation of God, the way in which Jesus distinguishes himself from the Father discloses that there is an eternal relationship of Father and Son in God. Jesus' self-distinction from God manifests the eternal self-differentiation of the Son from the Father which corresponds to the self-differentiation of the Father from the Son; and this, for Pannenberg, is the key for a correct interpretation of the cross of Christ.[21]

However, even if we accept this move from the historical fact of Jesus' obedient attitude to the God he called Father to the eternal mutuality of self-differentiation between Father and Son, we are still left with a binitarian rather than trinitarian account of God. Only when we move from the cross to the resurrection do we get an adequate understanding of the third person, for the resurrection, not the cross, 'depicts the dependence of the Father and the Son on the Spirit as the medium of their community'.[22] Accordingly Pannenberg describes the three persons as three mutually dependent centres of activity and not as three modes of being in one subject.

This conception of the Trinity has a number of important consequences: it dissolves the traditional Western distinction between immanent and economic relation in so far as 'the mutual self-differentiation of Father, Son and Spirit in the divine economy must be seen as the concrete form of the immanent trinitarian relations'.[23] Moreover, the 'mutuality of their active relationships implies for Pannenberg . . . that the *monarchia* of the Father has to be understood as the result of the cooperation of all three persons'[24] in the divine economy. 'From this perspective the world as a whole can be seen as the history in which it

---

[21] W. Pannenberg, *Systematic Theology*, vol. I, Edinburgh: T & T Clark 1992, ch. 5.
[22] Schwöbel, p. 276.
[23] Ibid., p. 275.
[24] Ibid., p. 276.

will be finally demonstrated that the trinitarian God is the only true God.'[25]

However, this claim about the eschatological vindication of the Trinity leaves Pannenberg with a problem which he fails to solve. If the full realization of the *monarchia* of the father is the Kingdom and if this is brought about only as the final result of the cooperation of all three persons in history, the divine unity of these three centres of activity is hidden and obscure in the course of history. Pannenberg emphasizes the 'eschatological resolution of the tension between the persons of Father, Son and Spirit in revelation and the hiddenness of the unity of God in the world'.[26] But – as Christoph Schwöbel has rightly pointed out – 'the question is how the three persons of the Trinity can be understood as presenting one divine essence without reducing them to moments or aspects of the one essential Godhead and without positing the divine essence as a fourth subject lurking behind the persons of Father, Son, and Spirit'.[27] It is here that Pannenberg's account fails most conspicuously. He does not succeed in offering a trinitarian solution to the problem of the unity of God which is more than an eschatological postponement. Rather he gets stuck in a dualist cul-de-sac: on the one hand he develops the difference of Father, Son and Spirit from his account of revelation in terms of Jesus' self-distinction from the God he calls father; on the other hand he grounds the unity of God in a metaphysical concept of God's essence prior to and independent of revelation: the concept of God as Infinite. This concept of God, at which we can arrive independently of revelation as Pannenberg is at pains to show,[28] is normative and regulates all our thinking and speaking of God, including our accounts of the Trinity. For whatever we want to say about Father, Son and Spirit on the basis of revelation, it must accord with the fundamental idea of God as the Infinite.

4. It is here that Falk Wagner criticizes Pannenberg for not going far enough. He hopes to remedy the revelationist leftovers which he detects in Pannenberg by basing his account of the Trinity on a theory of the absolute in the tradition of Hegel and

---

[25] Ibid.
[26] Ibid., p. 277.
[27] Ibid.
[28] Pannenberg, *Systematic Theology*, ch. 2.

Wolfgang Cramer.[29] A convincing and tenable account of God, he argues, must start from the idea of the absolute and not from any particular event or understanding of God in history, tradition or religious consciousness. For unless what we say about God is grounded in a theory of the absolute, which gives content to the idea of God without recourse to religious consciousness and its varying conceptions of God, we shall not be able to distinguish our account of God from superstitious and irrational belief. On the other hand, the theory of the absolute must be such that it allows us to explain or make sense of the actual ways in which religious consciousness conceives God. Wagner hopes to achieve this by describing God as the process of absolute self-determination, i.e. as the self-determination which determines itself to determine itself. This presupposes an internal differentiation of God into that which determines itself, that which can be determined by itself and that which is the self-determination of the self-determinable by the self-determinator. And he understands this threefold distinction as a conceptual reworking of the difference between Father, Son and Spirit. Hence he claims to have shown that before we turn to analysing revelation or any other event or fact of religion, we can, in purely rational or conceptual terms, arrive at a theory of the absolute which is intrinsically trinitarian in structure and character: the Trinity may be a mystery of faith, but it is rationally transparent to philosophical reason.

Even without going into a detailed discussion of Wagner's position it will be obvious that some very hard questions must be asked as to his understanding of reason, rationality, conceptual construction and, in particular, his view of the working of language and the translatability of the figurative language of faith into the conceptuality of a theory of the absolute. All this invites a number of well known Wittgensteinian criticisms. Nevertheless, the problem which he seeks to tackle is a real one: the doctrine of the Trinity is only an adequate doctrine of God if it is more than a mere expression and manifestation of Christian tribalism. It must be construed to provide an account of

---

[29] F. Wagner, *Was ist Religion? Studien zu ihrem Begriff und Thema in Geschichte und Gegenwart*, Gütersloh 1986, pp. 570ff; 'Theo-Logie. Die Theorie des Absoluten und der christliche Gottesgedanke', in H. Radermacher et. al., *Rationale Metaphysik. Die Philosophie von Wolfgang Cramer*, vol. II, Stuttgart 1989, pp. 216–55.

God – not of a Christian God (whatever that may be) or of some particular beliefs about Father, Son and Spirit which Christians (but not Jews and Moslems) happen to hold over and above their common belief in God. The God of Christian faith is not a particular Christian God but God as experienced and worshipped by Christians. And a doctrine of the Trinity will be inadequate if it fails to make this clear.

I have earlier noted that *anti-theism* is a common motif of trinitarian theology today. After the brief survey of Jüngel, Moltmann, Pannenberg and Wagner we can now add a second major motif: its *christological orientation*, i.e. its focus on the history of Jesus and, in particular, the nature of the involvement of God with the death of Jesus upon the cross. In a certain sense this is even true of Wagner who seeks to show that what Christians confess about God in the light of the death and resurrection of Jesus Christ is a universal truth about God, accessible not only to faith but also to reason.

Now what I want to suggest is that both the anti-theism and the christological orientation of trinitarian theology today are due to, and are a by-product of, the eschatological re-orientation of theology in our century. This brings us to the second step of my argument.

II.

I have spoken of the recovery of the eschatological dimension in twentieth century theology. The achievement is by no means unambiguous. Its most obvious result is that the 'terms "eschatology" and "eschatological" can . . . make their appearance in every conceivable kind of context and be applied in a bewildering variety of senses'[30]. Sometimes, as critics have complained, even 'an attempt is made to give the term *eschaton* a sense which it has never possessed and can never possess', in particular when it is applied to 'events which are not the end of history, and therefore not eschatological in any true sense of the word'.[31] Properly understood, they say, eschatology has to do with *ta*

---

[30] G. W. H. Lampe, 'Early Patristic Eschatology', in: *SJTh, OP* 2, 1957, pp. 17ff, p. 17.

[31] A. W. Argyle, 'Does "Realized Eschatology" Make Sense?', *HibJ* 51, 1953, pp. 385ff, 386.

eschata which happen just before the end of this age and the beginning of the next age.

Now whatever may be the proper sense of the word, it is true that the term 'eschatology' originally made its appearance in a specific dogmatic context and hence acquired a specific meaning.[32] It began its life in the seventeenth century as a technical term of Lutheran dogmatics (J. Gerhard, A. Calov). There it was used as title of the final section of the doctrinal exposition of the Christian faith, also entitled 'De novissimis' or 'Of the Last Things', which discussed such topics as death, resurrection, last judgement, eternal life and the consummation of the world. However, what became decisive for its theological career was the creative ambiguity build into this term. This is clearly illustrated by an English treatise published in London in 1649: 'Of the Four Last and Greatest Things, Death, Judgement, Heaven, and Hell'[33]: The four *eschata* mentioned here are not only said to be 'last' in the chronological sense of that which all of us must expect at some future time, they are also called 'greatest' in the sense of being of ultimate importance in and for our present life. Accordingly eschatology is not simply an appendix to dogmatics which describes some future events that are in principle beyond our present life and knowledge. It discusses the fundamental normative orientation of our present life in terms of its final end and ultimate points of reference. In this sense it is of import for the whole of dogmatics. For by presenting our life as destined to find its fulfilment and completion in God, it introduces a perspective into the Christian theological picture which affects, or should affect, all areas of life and thought.

Now it is true that in the orthodox period *ta eschata* were mostly treated as 'last' more in a chronological sense and less in an ultimate sense which would affect the rest of the theological corpus. But it needed only a slight change of emphasis for eschatology to take on the more fundamental meaning. Historically this took place towards the end of the nineteenth century when Johannes Weiss, Franz Overbeck and Albert Schweitzer re-

---

[32] S. Hjelde, *Das Eschaton und die Eschata. Eine Studie über Sprachgebrauch und Sprachverwirrung in protestantischer Theologie von der Orthodoxie bis zur Gegenwart*, München 1987.
[33] Abbot, 'The Literature of the Doctrine of a Future Life', in W. R. Alger, *The Destiny of the Soul. A Critical History of the Doctrine of a Future Life*, vol. II, New York 1968, p. 865.

discovered the thoroughly eschatological nature of Jesus' teaching and the unbridgable gap between his eschatological orientation and later Christianity. But while for some the term 'eschatology' came thus to be confined to a factual description of ancient views which are no longer tenable and which make no contribution to our modern understanding of the universe and God, Karl Barth – under the impact of the First World War – drew just the opposite conclusion and flatly declared that 'Christianity which is not entirely and completely eschatology . . . is entirely and completely contrary to Christ'.[34] Hence everything in theology had to be placed in an eschatological perspective – not just the traditional *eschata*.

The shift of meaning in the term eschatology which this occasioned has dominated the discussion in our century. Its gist can briefly be summarized: *From the* eschata *to the* eschaton, *and from the* eschaton *to the* eschatos.

The first move is characteristic of Tillich's writings on eschatology.[35] In the twenties he programmatically replaced talk of the *eschata* by talk of the *eschaton*. His reason is that eschatology has to deal not with 'things' that will take place at some future time, but with the ultimate meaning of everything insofar as it is historical being moving towards an end. This end is not another event in the series of events, but the transcendent destiny of beings in history. Hence he defines the *eschaton* as the 'transcendent meaning of historical being' ('transzendenter Geschehenssinn'),[36] a meaning that cannot be spelled out in temporal terms but is equally close to every moment of history where it manifests itself in completion and ultimate decision that leads to fulfilment. However, if 'in the *eschaton* there is nothing which is not in history',[37] as Tillich says, it is clear that the eschatological symbols of religious faith like life after death, last judgement, resurrection etc. are to be interpreted existentially rather than temporally or cosmologically. Only this will bring out their universal significance, and only by correlating history and the *eschaton* in this way will it be possible for

---

[34] K. Barth, *Der Römerbrief* (1922), Zurich 1967, 298 (Eng. trans. E. C. Hoskyns, *The Epistle to the Romans,* Oxford 1933, 314).

[35] P. Tillich, 'Eschatologie und Geschichte', *Die christliche Welt* 41, 1927, col. 1034ff.

[36] Ibid., col. 1035.

[37] Ibid., col. 1040.

theology to claim the ultimate unity of history and the history of salvation.

Tillich's attempt to recast eschatology in existential terms became widely influential. But it was also criticized for not going far enough. 'To eschaton (neuter) is not actually a New Testament phrase', it was objected. 'Loyalty to the Christocentric nature of all New Testament theology would require us to speak always of ho eschatos – not the last Thing, but the last Man', i.e. Jesus Christ.[38] He is the eschatos and the enactor of the eschaton. Hence we must move beyond Tillich's existential reinterpretation to a christological reworking of eschatology. This is what Tillich's teacher Martin Kähler had already originated; it was monumentally executed by Barth; and many have followed their lead. But if eschatology is the doctrine of the eschatos, it becomes virtually co-extensive with Christology and, as such, shapes Christian theology as a whole. Eschatology now has only one topic and subject matter: Jesus Christ, his life and message, cross and resurrection, and the soteriological implications of all this for our human existence and the whole of creation. So what theology must expound is not a series of eschatological topoi but the one eschatological reality of the risen Christ. This is bound to show in its account of God which now becomes – as I have claimed – necessarily trinitarian in character. Why and in which sense – these are the questions to which I turn in my third and final section.

III.

It has become a commonplace in much contemporary theology that the life of Jesus, his death and resurrection 'are eschatological events in the full sense; that is to say, they are . . . unique and final events, in which the God beyond history intervened conclusively to reveal His Kingdom on earth'.[39] However, this is by no means self-evidently so. Christians confess Jesus to be the Christ, the Lord or the Son of God who definitely disclosed and communicated God's self-giving love for his creation because, as they insist, the Spirit opened their eyes to this eschatological reality. Unless we come, through the power of the Spirit, to see

---

[38] J. A. T. Robinson, In The End God. A Study of the Christian Doctrine of the Last Things, London: SCM Press 1958, p. 56.
[39] C. H. Dodd, History and the Gospel, London 1938, p. 35.

and accept Jesus' life, death and resurrection as the true account
of our human situation before God and of God's loving attitude
towards us, we are blind to its eschatological nature and unable
to share its eschatological perspective: we cannot discern it as
the unique and final event in which God conclusively reveals his
Kingdom on earth. However, where it occurs it involves a far-
reaching reconstruction of our understanding of ourselves, of God
and of our reality in terms of the fundamental eschatological
contrast between *old* and *new:* the old life of our existence in
servile, distorted, destructive patterns in the past and the new
life in a community of reciprocal love and complementary service, whose potential horizons are universal and in which we
come to be what God wants us to be: free and perfect mirrors of his
goodness and love. Thus according to the Christian faith true,
i.e. salvific knowledge of God, Christ, our human situation and
the destiny of creation is rooted in the resurrection and results
from being drawn into the salvific presence of God's love by the
power of the Spirit.

This self-disclosing and self-communicating presence of God's
creative love is the complex eschatological reality to which
Christian theology refers. It is eschatological in the sense of
being the final and ultimately true reality in which and through
which we all have our being. Three features are essential to its
eschatological character: it is *divinely constituted*; it is *christologically determined*; and it is experienced as the *break-in of
radical newness in our life.* Individually and together these
three features give rise to a trinitarian account of God.

(1) Ontologically and epistemologically the eschatological,
i.e. final and ultimately relevant reality confessed by faith is
constituted by *God alone.* It is a complex act of God which discloses the true nature of God and of our created reality and of
which we can only become aware through God himself. Since it
is constituted by God *alone* all its aspects are entirely and exclusively due to God. Hence *that* it is (its *actuality*), *what* it is
(its *character*) and *that we (can) come to know* that and what it
is (its *intelligibility*) must be explained in terms of divine
activity; and since God *is* his activity and not something behind
or beyond it, this requires a trinitarian account of God. For if the
actuality, character and intelligibility of the eschatological
reality are due to God alone, it is the product of a complex divine
act which comprises the three fundamental sub-acts (variously

named in the dogmatic tradition) of creation, revelation (or redemption) and inspiration (or fulfilment) which together constitute divine activity.[40] That is to say:

– God constitutes the dependent reality and actuality of everything that is different from God (creation);

– God discloses the intention which governs his creative activity as love (revelation);

– God makes us see and accept that what he discloses in revelation about his love of creation is absolutely true and reliable (inspiration).

Thus just as without creation there is no revelation, and without revelation no inspiration, so without inspiration there is no awareness of revelation, and without this no awareness of creation. Hence creation, revelation and inspiration neither merely coexist nor coincide in an undifferentiated way. They differ from each other by the way they are related: whereas inspiration presupposes revelation and creation, creation achieves its end in inspiration through revelation; and they are related by distinguishing themselves from each other in such a way that created reality is allowed time and space to realize its potentiality and achieve its end in relative autonomy. This ordered relationship between creation, revelation and inspiration is what characterizes eschatological reality. Together the three basic types of divine activity constitute the one divine activity which allows time and space for everything to become what it will ultimately be. These three basic types of divine activity cannot be reduced to something more basic without dissolving divine activity altogether, and they cannot be ascribed to three different agents without destroying the unity and uniqueness of divine activity. Hence, if we want to be true to the eschatological reality experienced in the risen Christ, the unfathomable divine activity which we call God must be conceived as an internally differentiated field of activity with three centres of agency: the centre of creativity and reality (Father), the centre of intelligibility and truth (Son) and the centre of novelty and certainty (Spirit). These centres of activity are not different agents but 'three distinctive though internally related

---

[40] Chr. Schwöbel, 'Divine Agency and Providence', *Modern Theology* 3, 1987, pp. 225–44 ; 'Die Rede vom Handeln Gottes im christlichen Glauben', *Marburger Jahrbuch Theologie I*, 1987, pp. 56–81.

types of action'of the one divine activity'.[41] They are constituted through their relation to each other and hence constitute and structure divine activity as an internally differentiated process of self-constitution, self-organization and self-communication whose grammar is spelled out by the doctrine of the immanent Trinity.

(2) The second central feature is that the eschatological reality is intrinsically related to *Jesus Christ* (revelation). His life, death and resurrection reveal the character and point of divine activity to us: In his faithful and obedient relation to the God he called Father Jesus interpreted the basic character of God's radical creativity and unfailing closeness even in the face of sin and alienation to be unlimited paternal love towards us; and the foundational Christian experiences of the risen Christ proved, for Christians, that this interpretation, far from being falsified by the cross, has finally been vindicated: by resurrecting the crucified the Father acknowledged, confirmed and validated it as true account of his divine nature and will for the whole of creation; and through the power of the Spirit he makes believers accept this in faith. Hence Christians use the name 'Jesus Christ' to mark the generative eschatological rupture-experience which grounds the Christian faith, reveals the loving nature of God and discloses our ultimate destiny as human beings to be analogous to Jesus' death or to his resurrection depending on how we react to the love of God communicated to us in the Gospel.

Again this is reflected in the doctrine of the Trinity which for this reason speaks of the Son as well as of the Father: It is constitutive for the Christian understanding of God to refer not merely to absolute creativity but also to Jesus Christ who disclosed both that God is Father and that the character of his divine creativity is self-giving love. Through Jesus Christ we know that we can truly address God as Father and safely rely on the eschatological truth that the determinative character of divine activity is, and therefore was and will be, self-giving love. This christocentrism of all Christian thought about God has nothing to do with Christian tribalism. The 'Christian community has a focus for its identity in Jesus, yet the "limits" set by Jesus are as wide as the human race itself. The Christian

---

[41] Schwöbel, 'Divine Agency', p. 240.

"community" is potentially the whole world'.[42] Jesus sketched a new and comprehensive vocation for human beings, new possibilities for the form of human life as such, not merely for a particular group to find an identity. He did not proclaim a new deity but interpreted the nature of the only God there is in a new and definitive way to us. What we can see from Jesus is that God's creativity limits or determines itself in such a way that it allows time and space for created creativity to respond freely to it; and since we failed to do so, went to extremes to bring about our free response. It is important to see that this self-determination is not something additional or foreign to divine creativity but of its very essence and hence of universal validity. Therefore it was not improper to express it, by using the metaphors of Word, Image or Son, in terms of the eternal response and obedience of the Son. He not only shares in the divine creativity of the Father but, as he communicates to us through the Spirit, determines its nature to be unrestricted and inexhaustible love and hence, since all love hopes for reciprocity, the point and destiny of our human existence to respond to this divine love.

(3) The third central feature is that the eschatological reality breaks into our life as a radical rupture which shatters the continuities of our life (inspiration). Wherever it occurs, it ruptures the experiential and linguistic structures of our previous orientation in the world, disrupts our ways of perceiving and participating in reality, and establishes a fundamental difference between the old life and the new: the old, self-centred life in conflict with our human destiny as God's creatures and the God-centred new life in accordance with it. The latter is not a mere theoretical possibility of some future life. Rather the continuing exigencies of life after the occurrence of God's eschatological self-presentation force us to re-orient ourselves and our whole view of reality in the light of this rupture-experience here and now. Disorientation gives way to new orientation both in the individual life of faith and the life of the Christian community when, in Jesus Christ and through the Spirit, we become aware that the absolute gratuity, radical creativity and inexhaustible newness of God's love is the ultimate source and destiny of all there is. This radical re-orientation is aptly expressed as 're-birth' or 'new creation' because it is in no way

---

[42] R. Williams, 'Trinity and Revelation', *Modern Theology* 2, 1986, pp. 197–212, p. 202.

effected by us but, when it occurs, affects everything we are and do. We cannot even become aware of the divine constitution and saving character of the eschatological rupture-event without experiencing this as a gift from God, i.e. his illumining our minds and hearts to accept Jesus Christ as the living parable of God's love towards us. Moreover, this awareness is not merely a theoretical, but fundamentally a practical matter: it cannot occur, as Paul and many others show, without conversion, i.e. without redirecting a person's whole life in the light of the eschatological contrast between Old and New, between what is the case and what can, should and will be the case if we respond to God's love.

Again the doctrine of the Trinity reflects this. Reference to the radical eschatological rupture which resists assimilation to given structures of experience and language is one of its essential ingredients. It is encapsulated in the idea that God the Father is not generated, but purely generative, the ultimate, and ultimately unfathomable, source of all there is. But in talking of God the Son the doctrine of the Trinity also reflects that the creative eschatological rupture of all previous experience gives rise to a specific re-ordering of and re-orientation in reality, a new life in response to the paternal love of God disclosed in Christ. Thus both incomprehensible *creativity* and comprehensible *love* are central features of the Christian understanding of God. However, there is a further central aspect of Christian experience which it reflects: in re-ordering one's life in the light of the eschatological rupture, creativity and love are experienced not as contradicting but as mutually illuminating each other: love is discerned as the character of creativity and creativity as the nature of love. So the third central feature of the Christian understanding of God is its attempt to be true to the experience of permanent *progress towards novelty* due to the unfathomable creativity of love in which divine incomprehensibility and comprehensibility combine to determine God as the loving and inexhaustible advent of *newness* in human life and creation. This is why the doctrine of the Trinity does not merely speak of the Father and of the Son but also of the Spirit: it thus integrates into a complex pattern of divine activity the eschatological experience of incomprehensible divine creativity, comprehensible divine love and radical newness brought about by the inexhaustible creativity of divine love. The Spirit has priority over Son and Father in the order of experiencing eschatological reality in that he enables us to confess that Jesus is the Christ and that God truly is love. But he can only be identified as divine Spirit because of his essential relation to the Son who discloses the divinity of the Father to be saving love. And just as the doctrine of the procession of the Son from the Father safeguards the concrete determination of God as father and love, so the *filioque* safeguards the determination of the Spirit as the presence of *God* – a determination absolutely essential for discerning the Spirit.

The doctrine of the Trinity, then, clearly reflects the three central features of eschatological reality which I have identified. It seeks to safeguard the eschatological anchorage, christological determination and radical openness for novelty of all Christian talk and thought of God. Far from obscuring our understanding of God by turning God into an incomprehensible mystery, it continuously refers us back to the one place where the incomprehensible God has become comprehensible: the eschatological rupture-experience of the risen Christ. But it also insists that we must never confuse our ideas of God with the living God himself who is comprehensible only in so far as he makes himself comprehensible as Father, Son and Spirit. All our ways of talking to and about God in prayer, confession, proclamation and theological reflection serve as ways of taking of *God* only insofar as they reflect the eschatological rupture-experience of God's self-revelation which resists assimilation to the available symbolic structures. We achieve this at the symbolic level by means of negation ('God is not . . .') and qualification ('God is like . . . but . . .'), i.e. by qualifying the models we use (lord) in such a way that the irreducible difference between God and our world of experience is safeguarded (almighty lord). Anselm formulated the principle underlying this procedure of pointing to the incomprehensible in and through the comprehensible as the rule that whatever model we use in talking and thinking about God, what we say and think will ultimately be beyond intelligibility because God is greater than anything that can be thought, said or conceptualized. If 'God is finally a mystery, our conceptual grasp of him will take us only part of the way'.[43] That is to say we must qualify all our ways of thinking and talking of God in such

---

[43] J. Macquarrie, *In Search of Deity: An Essay in Dialectical Theism*, London: SCM Press 1984, pp. 25–6.

a way that the irreducible difference between our symbolic conceptualizations of God and the God whom we attempt to conceptualize is clearly marked.

However, while Anselm's rule helps us to observe the dialectic between comprehensibility and incomprehensibility in our thought about God, it stresses the strand of incomprehensibility at the expense of comprehensibility by disregarding the specific origin of this dialectic in Christian thinking and speaking: the eschatological rupture-experience in Jesus Christ on which all Christian talk and thought of God ultimately rests. This does not dissolve the strand of divine incomprehensibility. But neither does it leave us without an inkling as to what it means to be God. Rather it specifies God's comprehensibility in christological terms, i.e. by reference to the life, death and resurrection of Jesus Christ: what is comprehensible of God is what we come to learn about his creative love and our created existence through Jesus Christ and the Spirit.

It follows that theological accounts of God cannot come to grips with the dialectics between divine comprehensibility and incomprehensibility in terms of the rule of analogy that no likeness can be discerned between God and the created order without a greater unlikeness having to be discerned as well. On the contrary, what it needs in order to make sense of Christian talk of God is to specify rules which show how our various figurative and conceptual ways of talking of God can be related to, and must be re-translated into, the discourse of faith about the eschatological reality of the risen Christ. Only in this way will we be able to ensure that incomprehensibility will not prevail over comprehensibility in our thought about God. Not its reformulation in terms of an abstract theistic conception of God and its respecification in terms of a doctrine of analogical predication is the way to make sense of our theological concepts and doctrines of God but their interpretative re-translation into th e story of Jesus Christ and the discourse of faith of the Christian community.

To help us to achieve this is precisely the point of the doctrine of the Trinity which Nicholas Lash has aptly termed 'the "summary grammar" of the Christian account of the mystery of salvation and creation'.[44] It insists that all Christian uses of

---

[44] Lash, op. cit., p. 183.

'God' are to be determined by the eschatological rupture-experience to which the gospel of Jesus Christ testifies and which we come to accept as true by the working of the Spirit. It thus insists on the concreteness of all our talk of God – a concreteness which resists all attempts at generalizing our notion of God as a principle of whatever sort. This is reflected by the trinitarian rule that no general terms are to be used of Father, Son and Spirit. Not even 'person' (or an equivalent term) can be used of them in exactly the same way. So the trinitarian rule that all our talk of God has to be referred back to the eschatological experience of the risen Crucified does not dissolve the dialectic of comprehensibility and incomprehensibility in our understanding of God. But the former dominates the latter, and God's saving activity, manifest in the story of Jesus Christ, communicated to us in the Gospel, and made evident to us through the working of the Spirit provides a definite orientation for the Christian life in the world.

Therefore the doctrine of the Trinity is not merely the summary grammar of Christian talk and thought about God. It is the regulative framework of the whole Christian life. By distinguishing and relating, on the basis of the eschatological experience of the risen Crucified, Father, Son and Spirit in the way it does, it offers an integrating pattern for all aspects of Christian life, experience, thought and action. Thus:

– the Father-Son relationship represents and summarises not only the historical relationship of Jesus to the God he called father. It also reminds us of the irreplaceable role of Israel's God-experience in the Christian understanding of God and of the soteriological role of Jesus' story as the eschatological paradigm of our story.

– Similarly the Son-Spirit relationship represents and summarizes not only the experiential basis of our confession of Jesus as the Christ. It also insists that the identity of the Spirit as the Spirit of God depends crucially on his being determined by the relation to Jesus Christ. Unless God is intelligibly mediated to us (in Jesus Christ) and directly present to us (as Spirit) he cannot be known and addressed as God. And it finally reminds us that only because the Christian community or church is essentially determined by both the story of Jesus and the working of the Spirit, it can rightly claim to be the place where God is known and worshipped as he truly is.

– Finally, the Father-Spirit relationship represents and summarizes not only the ultimate ground for our confession of Jesus as the Christ. It also reminds us that God is not only at work in Israel and the church but everywhere in creation, albeit in an often indeterminate and unspecifiable way: God is not the private deity of the Christians but the Lord of all there is – whether this is known and acknowledged or not and even though it is only in and through Christ that his lordship is known and discerned as the saving power of love.

In short, then, the doctrine of the Trinity is the supreme symbolic summary of the grammar of the Christian perspective on God, world, human existence and history, and everything else – a perspective which is grounded in the eschatological experience of the risen Christ. By permanently referring us back to these roots it safeguards the concreteness, historical contingency, christological determination, universal inclusiveness and radical openness for novelty of the Christian perspective. Hence the function of this doctrine in Christian thought and theology is primarily regulative and corrective. It does not describe a mysterious transcendent reality but summarizes an understanding of God, world and human existence which is grounded in faith's experience of the risen Christ as the ultimate disclosure of God's creative activity of saving love. This is the primordial eschatological reality which grounds everything else. Unless we start from here, the regulative doctrine of the Trinity cannot be justified as a reliable account of God. Thus theological justifications of this doctrine will have to be in terms of an ontology of God's creative, saving and transforming activity of love.[45] This ontology is not a descriptive conceptual account of divine activity as such. It is an attempt to spell out the conditions and presuppositions without which the eschatological experience of the risen Christ could not be true. And the summary of these conditions in terms of God is the doctrine of the Trinity.

IV.

Let me end my remarks on the eschatological grounding of the doctrine of the Trinity with two final observations:

---

[45] I. U. Dalferth, *Existenz Gottes und christlicher Glaube. Skizzen zu einer eschatologischen Ontologie*, München: Chr. Kaiser 1984.

(1) If the doctrine of the Trinity is understood along the lines proposed here, we can see that it is not a speculative theory about the inner life of God but a practical doctrine. It seeks to be true to the salvific and person-involving character of the eschatological experience of God in Christ by talking of God not in the theoretical (external) perspective of an observer but in the practical (internal) perspective of the believer. Hence the third person language in which it is coined is really misleading: it does not describe God but reminds us that God (as distinct from our conceptions of God) is either known in the mode of the second person or not at all. There is no knowledge of God worthy of the name that is not provoked by God making himself present to us; this presence must be mediated if we are to discern and survive it; but neither intelligible mediation on its own nor divine presence as such constitute knowledge of God: they do so only together. Now all three aspects of proper, i.e. salvific knowledge of God: divine initiative, directness and intelligible mediation, are combined in the Christian view of God as Father (God's initiative), Spirit (God's direct co-presence with us) and Son (God's intelligible mediation). For God, as Christians confess, has made himself present, and continues to make himself present, in Jesus Christ and through the Spirit. But we cannot become aware of God's salvific presence in Christ and co-presence with us in the Spirit without responding to it in doxology, prayer, confession and conversion. Thus direct and mediated knowledge of God as disclosed in Christ is to be had only by those who are enabled and guided by the Spirit to lead a life governed by the memory and the presence of Jesus. In so far as the doctrine of the Trinity spells out this internal doxological perspective on God, it talks of him in the mode of the second rather than the third person.

(2) It follows from this that the doctrine of the Trinity does not offer a concept of God but insists on the fundamental and irrevocable difference between God and all our models, ideas and concepts of God, between the creative reality of love which we call 'God' and our various figurative and conceptual attempts to talk to and of this divine reality. If Christians call Jesus God's revelation, then 'not because he makes a dimly apprehended God clear to us, but because he challenges and queries' our sense of God, because he 'represents the *immediacy* of divine presence

and creativity in the world, and thus the overthrow of our conceptual idols'.[46]

Accordingly, by insisting on the intrinsic reference of all Christian talk of God to the eschatological reality of God's self-communicating presence in Jesus Christ and through the Spirit, the doctrine of the Trinity has not a descriptive but a regulative function. It permanently reminds us that there is a fundamental difference between God and our conceptions of God; that God has disclosed himself in Jesus Christ as love so that there, and there alone, comprehensibility prevails over incomprehensibility; that without God's self-presentation and self-communication in Christ and through the Spirit we cannot re-orient our lives in the light of his love and hence come to know God in the sense required for salvation; and that we can never control the divine creativity of love disclosed in Christ but always must be open for the new and unexpected: God is not an incomprehensible mystery but comprehensible and experiencable as love, yet the creativity of his divine love is greater than anything we can conceive. God's love cannot be domesticated by us. It eludes all attempts at domestication by our symbols, models, concepts and codes of conduct. It is the inexhaustible mystery and unfathomable source and goal of all created being and its creative advance towards perfect realization. We see only darkly and in outline what this will involve by the eschatological pattern of Jesus' life, death and resurrection. But – and this is the ground and content of Christian hope – we believe his story to be the paradigm of all our stories, and the manifestation of God's love in his life to be the promise and confirmation of what will be true of our own and every life as well. For, to quote Paul, 'as in Adam all die, even so in Christ shall all be made alive'. We do not know how this will be achieved and what it will involve. But we have confident hope that the creative love which has become manifest in the eschatological reality of the risen Christ will continue its quiet work of transformation and achieve its end of turning creation into a free and perfect mirror of God's goodness and love.

[46] Williams, op. cit., p. 203.

Index of Subjects

compiled by Corinna Schlapkohl and Markus Mühling-Schlapkohl

171

Index of Authors